The Model's Handbook

The Model's Handbook

Julian Okines
and Fiona Brattle

THE CROWOOD PRESS

First published in 2011 by
The Crowood Press Ltd
Ramsbury, Marlborough
Wiltshire SN8 2HR

www.crowood.com

British Library Cataloguing-in-Publication Data
A catalogue record for this book is available from the
British Library.

ISBN 978 1 84797 300 9

Disclaimer
The author and publisher do not accept any
responsibility in any manner whatsoever for any error
or omission, or any loss, damage, injury, adverse
outcome, or liability of any kind incurred as a result of
the use of any of the information contained in this
book, or reliance upon it

Typeset by
Phoenix Typesetting, Auldgirth, Dumfriesshire

Printed and bound in Malaysia by
Times (Offset) M Sdn Bhd

Acknowledgements
Special thanks go to Michael Zammit and Andrew
Botten, personal trainers and friends, for all the exercise,
training and movement advice; to Elizabeth Walsh at
www.lovefoodforlife.com for taking time to out from
fashion show producing to help devise the Model Meal
Plan; to Laura Garrett for all her knowledge about make-
up and giving up her time to model for the beauty
shots; to Sally Kettle, photographer, model and trained
beauty therapist, for her skincare and body maintenance
tips; to James Granstrom for his superb knowledge of
Tokyo and the Japanese market; to Jennifer Fairbairns for
her colourful description of Athens.

Thanks to Kate Krause, Rebecca Palmer and Paul
Cavalier at www.nevsmodels.co.uk, Joe Tootal at
www.models1.co.uk, Natalie Kates at
www.qmodels.com, Benjamin Meier at
www.modelwerk.de, Lou Grima, Simon and Miranda
Cantacuzene-Speransky at www.stormmodels.com and
the whole team at www.icemodels.co.za; all of whom
offered thoughts on getting the most out of the
relationship with your booker, helped with travel and
visa information and getting image use approval,
answered questions and showed unwavering support.
A big thanks to Grace Chorley at
www.associationofmodelagents.org – your time and
advice were priceless.

We would like to thank all who donated their time
and talent for the book's photography: Zak Gollop for
his fantastic food and travel photography; Caroline Von
Tuempling for her fantastic work and inspirational
locations; Cape Town's finest, Bryce Thompson;
Malcolm Griffiths for shooting the exercise photography
and beauty shots, as well as donating shots from his
portfolio and letting us use a shot of his beautiful baby
boy – Ted Griffiths; Alex Beer at for sharing his work
and fantastic tattoos; Ryan Barrett for inspiring the
front cover design and shooting it and not forgetting
Tommy Clarke, Archie Adams, Paul McDougal, Fanie
Nel, Shape Magazine, Roger Wells, Eddie Macdonald
for their irreplaceable work. Furthermore, a big thanks
to Maryam Hamizadeh and the Clothes Show Live team
for allowing us the use of their press shots. Lastly, a
massive thank you to all the featured models – we
know how precious a commodity you are!

Contents

What the Agents Have to Say . . .

The Model's Handbook is a comprehensive guide and, as well as providing informed career advice, the book includes information and insights on a wide range of topics, including health, beauty, travel, finance, agents, self-esteem, and handling rejection in style.

The brainchild of two highly professional and successful models, this book provides a rare insight into our industry. It will become an invaluable tool for all working models; people who wish to build a career in modelling and young girls and guys everywhere.

Sarah Doukas, founder of Storm Models

The Model's Handbook is just what the industry needs. If all models took heed of the advice shared by Julian and Fiona, everyone involved in the business would benefit beyond imagination.

Steffi Freier, founder and director of Ice Models, South Africa

Modelling is a one hundred mile an hour business and the advice offered in The Model's Handbook will help every model learn how to handle life in the fast lane.

Joe Tootal, booker at Models1

Working as a model is a lot harder than most think. Unless you learn to switch on, play the game and look after yourself you're not going to last. The Model's Handbook will help you from day one and guide you to wherever you want modelling to take you.

Even models who have been working for years can improve their chances with the advice within.

Paul Cavalier, director of Nevs Models

Modelling can be a fantastic lifestyle as long as you understand that it is a job and modern clients will not tolerate unprofessionalism. The Model's Handbook can help you achieve success, job satisfaction and understand the unique psychology of working as a fashion model.

John Bruce, women's booker at Premier Model Management

Introduction

I can walk into a room full of people I don't know and do my job. That's quite a massive thing to learn.

Kate Moss

To prepare for the clients of tomorrow, today's model needs to understand that there is more to the job than just posing for photographs or walking down the runway. By appreciating how the system works, the time and effort involved, and why it has been shaped this way, you can offer a lot more than the stereotypical view of a model might suggest. Start by examining the way a company reaches out to the consumer and you'll see a good model doesn't have an inflated ego. Instead, a good model appreciates that the focus of any shoot, show or commercial is not on them but on the story being told and the product being sold. In short, the role of a professional model is to act as the advertiser's ambassador as they paint a portrait of perfection.

HOW THE INDUSTRY WORKS

CONCEPT

Initially, when an advertiser is trying to promote a particular product, brand or service, they must devise a concept that connects with their chosen demographic. This responsibility lies primarily with the company's in-house marketing department or an affiliated advertising agency. Using market research, clever thinking and artistic flair, they attempt to create a desirable, successful or life-affirming image that resonates with the wants and needs of the consumer. Once this abstract idea has formed, the project is entrusted to a producer, creative director, photographer and stylist, who then assume the responsibility of realizing the vision.

CASTING

The focus then shifts to selecting the right featured artists for the project. Model agencies and casting directors are contacted and various models' promotional materials are viewed. The client may also explain the personality most likely to suit their needs. Then, a few days or weeks before the shoot or show, a selection of models are invited to attend a casting for the job.

From those present at the casting, the client creates a shortlist of models and places them on option. Then, depending on availability, negotiable rates, the dynamic of the group or simply who is the best model for the job, the option is either upgraded to a confirmation or taken off completely. Elsewhere the final preparations for the project take place and make-up artists, set designers, hairstylists, digital assistants and a whole host of others are hired to ensure the production's success.

COMPLETION

On the actual day of the shoot or show, the preparation is finally put to the test and, if all goes as planned, the client should feel confident that the concept has been achieved. However, each project is unique: locations, weather, on-set chemistry and stress can all throw up surprises that the artists and crew have to deal with. Therefore, as a model, you have to be prepared for all possibilities, be able to adapt to various situations, and under no circumstances be the cause of any problems on set. Models may operate at the more glamorous end of this industry, but they are, nevertheless, cogs in a machine that utilizes the expertise of countless others. Appreciating the amount of time and effort spent on bringing a concept to life will help you to achieve a lot more.

After filming or shooting, when a model's work is seemingly done, the raw material is compiled in post-production and readied for the marketplace. Photographic retouching by digital artists is, today, an industry standard, and the finished article can look very different to the image captured on the shoot day. There are also promotional considerations, press releases and follow-up campaigns, which are all organized by PR agencies. These may entail models having additional commitments to promote or even represent the brand once it is available to the public.

Once exposed to the public, a concept will be judged by its commercial success and although this can impact on your career, your focus should remain on securing repeat business with tools you have control over. Your look, your book and your attitude are all firmly in your grasp and are the keys to your success. By remaining versatile, humble and focused, you can capitalize on any initial successes and enjoy a long, varied and financially rewarding career as a professional model.

MODELLING: PAST, PRESENT AND FUTURE

Modelling can be a lucrative and exciting lifestyle but just a brief glance at the history of the fashion and advertising industry highlights how the demands of the job have changed over the last twenty years. Back then, a handful of supermodels enjoyed the attentions of the top brands in the world, which clambered over each other to secure their services. Moreover, these clients were willing to pay for the privilege; leading model Linda Evangelista was famously quoted in *Vogue* as saying: 'We don't wake up for less than $10,000 a day.' However, the landscape is currently very different and various factors have enabled advertisers to maximize their message's exposure whilst minimizing production budgets. Meanwhile, the number of boys and girls hoping to make it in the fashion world has exploded. This means there are more models working for less money.

The story of how our industry has changed since the start of the new millennium undoubtedly begins with the rise of the Internet. Previously, advertisers were only able to showcase their product, brand or service in print or on film. Then, almost overnight, advertising went digital, and with it came new ways to reach the consumer. Viral advert campaigns, emailed newsletters, social networking sites, pop-ups, videos and the company's own web page suddenly offered global access to the consumer at a fraction of the cost of television, magazines or the high street. With the awareness of a much broader, inexpensive and pressure-free environment in which to advertise, clients were no longer constrained by traditional methods and this was reflected in the rates that models could charge for their services.

Meanwhile, agency websites allowed detailed access to their models' composite cards, digital portfolios, videos and up-to-date polaroids. Photographs no longer had to be couriered, the need to see models in the flesh was reduced and, coupled with a sharp decline in the cost of air travel, advertisers were offered an unlimited supply of boys and girls throughout the world. In short, different markets were no longer exclusive to the models who worked within them and, again, this resulted in lower day rates for all.

The Internet also allowed more agencies to emerge, whereas before an agency had to be situated in the heart of a country's fashion capital, with an expensive office and highly paid bookers. Now, dwindling physical contact between agencies and potential clients permit agencies to be run from small offices, with few overheads and for a fraction of the cost. However, their websites remain glamorous and luxurious, blurring the distinction between the higher-calibre agencies and those prepared to negotiate unfairly low rates for their models.

A change in photography further highlighted the shift towards the digital age. Previously, film photography required a slow, well-crafted process, where the client placed immense trust in both the photographer and model to ensure the finished product was exactly as planned. However, digital cameras now permit the client to closely monitor a production. Once confident the raw image is captured, the crew can move on to the next part of the brief and the process is so much faster than before, that the volume of shots expected in a day has increased many times over. Also, digital retouching can shape photographs to appear very different from the reality, thus opening the door for more boys and girls.

Meanwhile, despite the decline in rates, the instant fame generated by reality television, and a growing obsession with celebrity, mean more young girls and boys than ever are viewing modelling as a viable career.

This surplus of talent has meant that, for a large proportion of models, the job is only ever a part-time venture, requiring them to supplement their income with anything form bar work to personal training to club promoting. Furthermore, for these part-time models, the sporadic income offers little job satisfaction and after a couple of years they leave the industry behind, seeking financial security elsewhere. This high turnover of models has led to an industry that feels as though it is in constant flux: agencies recruiting new faces to replace those who have moved on and clients being offered a larger pool of less professional models than they perhaps would prefer.

The good news is that there are still advertisers willing to spend money on good quality models if they believe that they will reap the eventual benefits. It is the responsibility of all models to raise the standard by being more professional and understanding the needs of the client without the need to compromise rates.

Remember: you don't have to be a supermodel to be a super model.

1 : New Faces

Self-love has very little to do with how you feel about your outer self. It's about accepting all of yourself. You've got to learn to accept the fool in you as well as the part that's got it going on.

Tyra Banks

This chapter aims to teach you how the fashion industry works and the many different ways in which models are used. Once you get to grips with the basics and consider whether a career in modelling is right for you, you'll need to secure representation with a model agency. Although seeking representation may appear to be a daunting experience, it is relatively straightforward and by following the steps provided, you'll be able to make a good impression with the right people as well as avoiding costly scams. Once you sign your contract and make the transition from hopeful to 'new face', you can start to prepare for life as a professional model. One part of that preparation is knowing the truth about what really goes on in the industry. However, before you even consider a career as a model, you need to ask yourself, 'Have I got what it takes?'

HAVE I GOT WHAT IT TAKES?

This question does not immediately refer to your physical attributes because 'modelling' is such a broad term. A modelling job can be as simple as trying on a garment for a clothing company, to an all print, high street, television and cinema campaign requiring weeks to shoot. There are many different types of model just as there are many different types of consumer. For example, there are plus-size models, promotional models, sport and fitness models, glamour models, fit models, show models and many more. It is this variety, as well as its uniqueness, that makes modelling a viable career for a wider range of people than most would think. As long as you can consistently connect with a demographic, there will always be advertisers hoping to secure your services. Of course, if you are able to cover a range of different types of modelling, you are more likely to succeed.

Instead, the question 'Have I got what it takes?' is a call for you to examine your personality as well as your physical appearance, because whilst there are positives to being a model, there are also many daily stresses and strains that are frequently overlooked. For example, handling rejection, travelling constantly and overcoming people's preconceived notions about models are all challenges of the profession. A robust self-esteem, a positive outlook and being comfortable as the centre of attention are all character traits that you need.

One trait that is essential is the ability to judge your look objectively. This begins with an honest, but not overly critical, appraisal of your physical appearance. In the privacy of your own home, strip down to your underwear and examine your face and physique. Then, through unbiased eyes, consider the areas that would benefit you as a model, as well as those that perhaps might stand in your way. There are genetic fundamentals which are unlikely to change, such as your height once fully grown, your bone structure and facial characteristics. In contrast, there are environmental factors that can be worked on with a balanced diet, exercise, styling and make-up. These include your body shape, skin, hair and the image you present to the wider world.

Remember: making it in the modelling industry is as much about your personality as your physicality.

TYPES OF MODELLING

There are various ways you can make money as a model and understanding how to tap into these revenue streams can make the difference between success and failure. Fashion, high street, runway and commercial modelling can all be considered as 'above the line' work but are just the tip of the iceberg. There are also many jobs that are referred to as 'below the line' work that, although never seen by the wider public, still offer various financial opportunities. Add to these the more niche types of modelling and a picture emerges that

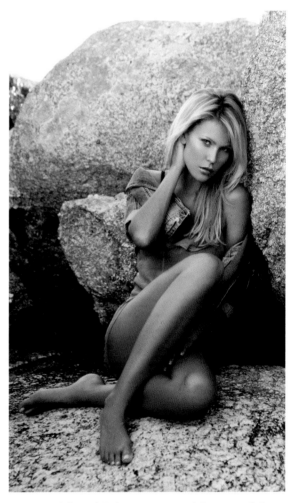

Commercial work is how most models earn a living, but the images can still be beautiful and complimentary to both model and photographer.

modelling is not just about being tall, good-looking and exuding sex appeal. If you are versatile enough to work with a range of clients and on differing projects, you can ensure that your career is both varied and lucrative.

ABOVE THE LINE
Commercial Versus Editorial
How commercial or editorial a model's 'look' is, simply refers to the demographic they appeal to, the type of product they sell and, therefore, the type of client and work they attract. If a 'commercial look' sits at one end of a scale, then an 'editorial look' sits at the other and all models feature somewhere in between. Ideally, a fashion

Editorial work earns the respect of the fashion community. The shoots are a little more edgy and perhaps a little more gritty.

I know a model who ...

booked a first class ticket at the client's expense. They paid for it, but deleted his number.

model should sit near the centre of the scale and be able to seamlessly make the transition between commercial and editorial. Supermodels achieve this perfect balance: they earn the respect of the more artistic portion of the industry whilst ensuring they are commercial enough to have financial security for life.

Most model agencies list requirements regarding height, age and measurements for any hopefuls considering a career. Firstly, height requirements are relatively strict and 1.73m (5ft 8in) is considered a minimum for girls. Boys should be between 1.83m (6ft) and 1.91m (6ft 3in). Falling short of these guidelines is not a disaster but limits a model's options and, therefore, their financial viability. Similarly, a few agencies will only consider representing new faces aged sixteen to twenty-one, but if an older girl wishes to break into the industry, there are still many opportunities for her to find representation.

NICHE MODELLING
Plus-size Modelling
There is a serious debate as to whether plus size modelling should be considered a niche part of the industry. It is currently one of the fastest growing areas in fashion and many top agencies are considering opening divisions dedicated solely to plus-size models. Typically, a plus-size model is female, has a larger bust and dress size than the average fashion model and more closely reflects the physique of the average consumer. A plus-size model can expect to work mostly for catalogues, for lingerie companies, in television commercials and in mainstream fashion shows. They need to be physically well proportioned and exude health, as well as be bursting with charisma and self-confidence.

Glamour Modelling
Glamour modelling is primarily for girls who are very comfortable being photographed in lingerie, swimwear

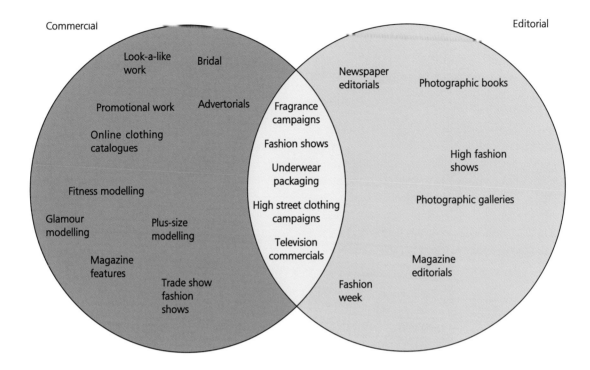

Commercial

Editorial

Look-a-like work

Bridal

Promotional work

Advertorials

Online clothing catalogues

Fitness modelling

Glamour modelling

Plus-size modelling

Magazine features

Trade show fashion shows

Fragrance campaigns

Fashion shows

Underwear packaging

High street clothing campaigns

Television commercials

Newspaper editorials

Photographic books

High fashion shows

Photographic galleries

Magazine editorials

Fashion week

The diagram above highlights the types of job you are likely to find, depending how commercial or editorial your look is.

or topless and behaving provocatively towards the camera. The destination of these shots is mainly newspapers and men's interest magazines. In addition, glamour girls can quickly attain a celebrity status, leading to personal appearances and merchandizing. Glamour modelling has no height restrictions and although a larger bust is preferred, many different body shapes are accepted. Girls considering a career in glamour modelling often opt to have breast enlargements.

There are many agencies dedicated solely to repre-

I know a model who ...

never shuts up about what they are doing or who they are working for. It's so exhausting.

Modelling is about connecting with the consumer, disproving the idea that you have to look a certain way to model.

With the right exercise and nutrition, you can shape your body in any way you choose.

Glamour modelling can be a fast track to fame.

senting glamour girls and although some models make the transition between glamour and fashion modelling, finding an agent who specializes in raising your profile as well as generating business can prove a lucrative combination. However, glamour girls need to be particularly protective of their image rights, especially if they hope to avoid being exploited. Similarly, although all models should avoid being captured in photographs they might later regret, glamour girls need to be especially careful. Shots featuring glamour girls are usually sexually explicit, but that is not a licence for a photographer to push boundaries, so always make sure that you stay in control.

Sport and Fitness Modelling

All models should be in good physical condition and an athletic physique can lead to sportswear and fitness bookings as a result. For boys, this usually means a large muscle mass and a level of definition that requires dedication. Female sports models usually have toned, healthy bodies and athletes sometimes branch into this area of the industry. However, it is important to not discount yourself from more mainstream work either by

I know a model who ...

refused to do overtime. She just said, 'I've had enough!' I was amazed.

Being an expectant mother is an exciting time of life and, for models, it can be a whole new chapter in their career.

losing a sense of femininity or by becoming too broad to fit into samples. There is plenty of work in the sports sector for a muscular physique but, for most clients, tone is preferred over size.

With the right exercise and nutrition, you can shape your body in any way you choose.

Maternity Modelling

When a woman is pregnant, there are no rules forbidding her from modelling. In fact, once she begins to show, there is an entire area of the industry that revolves around pregnancy and maternity photography. New mothers and newborns are also widely photographed. However, you don't have to be with child in order to be booked for pregnancy or maternity work and it is not uncommon for models to be asked to bond with a newborn on set or even be given a fake baby bump to wear.

Promotional Modelling

Promotional work is all about connecting with the consumer and usually uses a degree of theatricality to bring a product or brand to life. Therefore, promotional models need to be very engaging and full of personality; a good sense of humour always helps. Jobs can be as varied as greeting celebrities at a film premier to acting as a live mannequin in a shop window, and although rates are significantly lower than for mainstream modelling, there are a constant stream of events and clients available. Promotional agencies are always keen to sign up new faces.

I know a model who ...

is such a diva. She never gets repeat bookings.

BELOW THE LINE

Below the line work is just as varied as mainstream modelling and sourcing ways to generate additional revenue can be a real boost to your annual turnover.

Fit Modelling

Fit models are used in clothing production and should not be confused with fitness models. When a clothing company produces a garment, there is a standard process that begins with a simple design on paper and ends with the garment on sale in the high street. Once the aesthetics, dimensions and fabric of a design have been approved, a single garment is produced, which is known as a sample. The role of a fit model is to work with the designers and garment technicians to ensure that the sample has the right look, fit and quality. Typically, fit models are a similar size to mainstream fashion models, although there are small changes from brand to brand. Working as a fit model can be a good source of regular income, even if it represents the slightly less glamorous side of the fashion world.

Showroom Modelling

Once a clothing company has produced a range for the upcoming season, there are three different points of sale they can utilize: their own outlets, the Internet and department stores. The last option represents a great opportunity to reach a wide variety of consumers, and companies therefore invest a lot of time and money in convincing buyers from department stores to stock their clothing lines. One of the best ways to showcase the range to buyers is by having models wear a selection of garments during an informal catwalk show, usually held at the company offices or showroom.

Showrooms are quite an intimate environment, which makes getting on with the client just as important as looking good in the clothes. Prior to the buyers' arrival, ask questions about the range and any particular points or details you should highlight. During the meeting, the buyers may even ask you questions about the range or your opinion on the fit and feel of particular items, so be sure to answer promptly, favourably and intelligently. A good showroom client will book you frequently throughout the year and season after season.

Look Books

As well as using showroom models to appeal to buyers, clothing companies also present each season's range in the form of a look book. These are usually shot on a neutral background but can also have key outfits shot on locations, and these photos can make useful additions to a portfolio. There is also the possibility that the photographs can carry over onto the high street, which could mean an additional buyout. Therefore, when shooting look books, never sign a model release contract.

Corporate Videos

Corporate videos are purely for in-house purposes and can be anything from an instructional video to a short film about a product or service. They often pay well, but never sign away your image rights as it could cost you a buyout in the future.

In summary, there aren't different types of model, just different types of job. The more you can do, the more you will work. For example, a clothing company uses fit models during production, showroom models to pitch to buyers, catwalk models during its launch, fashion models for the high street campaign and magazines, and promotional models to connect directly with the consumer. Furthermore, each client is individual and has specific needs, making room for more niche types of modelling.

HOW MUCH MONEY DO MODELS EARN?

It is almost impossible to judge a model's earning potential. Although various standards regarding a model's time, image use and exposure exist within the industry, every model, agency and client is unique. For example, one model might get months of repeated bookings with a catalogue client, and earn the exactly same amount of money as a second model shooting an advertising campaign for just one day. Of course, if the first model books both jobs, then their annual income will be healthier as a result. Therefore, you should aim to convert as many castings into work as possible and with the right look, book and attitude, this is entirely possible. Eventually, the goal is to be in a position where you balance regular work with a handful of loyal clients, whilst still casting for one-off campaigns and high-profile work. Then, as your reputation and client base improves, your agent may decide to raise your rates. Eventually, with enough quality bookings and some careful money management, it is not rare for models to become extremely wealthy. However, whilst modelling can be a fun, lucrative and exciting lifestyle, it is a business with no guarantees. Every year your annual income starts at zero and it is up to you to improve that figure. Without giving your career constant care and attention, the chances of failure are just as real as your chance of being a success.

The first step in working out how much you could earn is understanding terms such as rates, usage and buyouts and what they mean for you. Although your agent is responsible for negotiating your fees, it is your time and image that are for hire and therefore your decision about whether to accept a job. The more jobs you accept, the more money you are likely to make. However, there are occasions when saying no to work can protect your reputation and the likelihood of long-term financial success.

INDUSTRY STANDARDS

Rates and Usage

Model's rates are initially calculated by the hour, half-day or day. Most bookings are for a minimum of two hours and a standard working day is considered to be eight to ten consecutive hours. Any hours worked in excess are usually billed as additional time and a half per hour; this is called overtime. However, day rates are frequently accompanied by usage buyouts for which the client must pay an additional fee. The amount of this buyout depends on duration of usage of the image, the number of territories in which it appears, the types of media in which an image is used and how prominently the model features. In addition, there are other variables that depend on the market, the client and their available budgets, the negotiating prowess of an agent and the perceived reputation and marketability of the model. Again, this highlights how hard it is to predict how much each model is likely to earn on a particular job, let alone over the span of their career.

Cancellations

Even after confirmations have gone ahead and contracts have been signed, cancellations can still occur. Cancellation policies differ from agent to agent, but, usually, a cancellation five working days prior to booking will require the client to pay half the agreed fee. A full fee is charged on jobs that are cancelled less than twenty-four hours before the shoot commences. In addition, cancellation of trips or full week bookings can result in the full fee being charged, so it is unlikely for a client to change their mind once an agreement is reached. It is also one of the reasons why castings are essential for models, as clients are extremely particular about where, and on whom, they spend their budget.

Model Release Contracts

On some jobs you may be presented with a model release contract at the end of a shoot. Under no circumstances should you sign a model release contract without consulting your agent. This is mainly because this contract states that the photographer or client will have exclusive use of all the images and are no longer required to either consult or compensate you for their use. Depending on the terms and conditions of the contract, this can be global and for an unlimited period of time. Models have lost huge sums of money by unwittingly signing model release contracts and forgoing their image rights. Almost as important as the loss of earnings is the possibility of your face being associated with either an unethical brand or an embarrassing or sexually explicit concept, further highlighting the need never to sign a model release contract without advice.

A library shoot is the most likely place a model will be presented with a model release contract because there is no set destination for the images. Even so, you should not sign this without your agent's approval. When a model release contract is presented to you, tell the client

> ## I know a model who ...
>
> shot a corporate video and signed a model release. A year later it was used in store and he missed out on £10,000.

to send a copy to your agency to be signed at a later date. If the client reminds you that you will not be paid until the model release contract is signed, then ask to take the contract away, go to your agency the following day and ask a booker or member of the accounts team to read over the contract with you. This way it can be amended, signed and sent with your invoice.

Voucher Books (America)

In Europe, when a model is confirmed on a job, the agency sends the client a contract stipulating the terms and conditions for the model's time and image usage, and then once the job is completed, an invoice is sent. As far as the model is concerned, all the financial aspects of the booking are handled by the agency bookers and accounts team. However, in America, although both the pre-confirmation contract and invoice are the responsibility of the agency, each model is required to present a form or voucher to the client at the end of each working day, confirming day rate, working hours and final invoice. Any overtime adjustments or last-minute changes can therefore be agreed by all parties and, more importantly, there is written proof of those changes. The voucher, which consists of three copies – a white copy for the client, a yellow copy for the agency and a pink copy retained by the model for their records – is then processed and the invoice can be sent. It is essential always to have a voucher book when arriving at a job, because, without written confirmation, the client can contest exactly what went on and how much you are owed. If you ever forget your voucher book, then borrow one from a fellow model or get the client to confirm the booking on paper.

Overtime and Expenses

How much you will receive is stipulated in the confirmation contract prior to the job, although any overtime, expenses or additional usage also need to be accounted for once the job is completed. Therefore, it is important to notify your bookers of any changes during the working day. Keep all your expense receipts and ensure you send them or scan and email them to your accounts team as soon as possible. Not all clients cover expenses, so check with your agent.

MODEL AGENCIES

Having assessed your credentials as a model, thought about your level of commitment and decided on which type of modelling you are best suited to, the next step is finding an agency to represent you. The role an agent plays in your career will affect its path, making it crucial to understand how an agency works and which agency will be most beneficial to your pursuit of modelling success. This is important if you hope to form a successful relationship and avoid those agencies that wish to exploit you.

Before you begin hunting for an agent, it is useful to know exactly how they operate. Model agencies exist all over the world and although each one has unique policies, represents individual models and operates in different types of market, they all are businesses and, like any business, they exist to generate a profit. This is done by proposing the models on their books to prospective clients and, if all goes as planned and the client agrees to use the model, the agency negotiates a fee and then charges the model a 20–25 per cent commission for services performed. In addition to the commission charged to the model, the agency will also charge the client a supplementary booking fee of 20 per cent. For example, in the USA, if a model charges a client $3,000 for a photo shoot, the invoice will be drawn up as: $3,000 + 20 per cent (meaning that the total bill is actually $3,600). From this total, the model will take $2,400 ($3,000 minus $600) and the agent will receive $1,200 ($600 from the model and $600 from the client). The booking fee is never seen by the model, and is an industry standard. Although at first glance this may seem excessive, considering the service an agency provides to both parties, it is wholly justifiable.

Although the structure of each model agency differs throughout the industry, an agency is always divided into divisions: a women's board, a men's board and a development board for new faces. Each division is staffed by a team of bookers, or booking agents as they are also known, with different bookers being primarily responsible for different clients and models. Some of the larger agencies are likely to have additional divisions, with bookers who handle television commercial clients, more mature or 'best age' models or specialist areas such as acting and presenting. The agency as whole is overseen by directors, who can also act as bookers.

At this point, it should be noted that some bookers are paid a salary by the agency, whilst others take an additional personal commission from the jobs they book. The main advantage of the commission system is that if you are not financially viable, then neither is your agent. However, an agency can have hundreds of models on their books and if an individual is not succeeding or is behaving in an unprofessional manner, bookers are unlikely to make special efforts on their behalf. Even for bookers who are paid a flat annual salary, irresponsible behaviour is frustrating.

Overall, your success is your agent's primary concern. And remember: you are not their boss and neither are they yours. Instead, they are a salesperson and you are the product; a good salesperson is limited by the standard of the product they are trying to sell and the product will never get sold without a good salesperson.

CHECKING IN

Personal chemistry may determine if your relationship with your booker develops into a friendship, but certain behaviour ensures it will at least be a professional and productive union. The bare minimum is to always 'check in' towards the end of each working day, either by phone or email. By doing this, your booker knows you to be available for the following day's castings or work, that the information is clear and that the client will be neither inconvenienced nor disappointed. Letting down clients or casting directors reflects badly on the individual model and the agency as a whole. Also, once you have been checked in, a process that takes less than a minute, your agent can effectively tick you off their to-do list and move on to the next model. This acts a courtesy to your fellow models and reinforces your reputation as a professional.

The best time to check in is during the last hour and a half of the day, although if you know yourself to be unavailable for any reason, check in early and ask your agent to inform you of any changes with an email or voicemail. If you have a chance to respond, then do so. Otherwise, call the next day as soon as your agency opens, let your booker know that you received the changes and that you are acting accordingly. Also, because this represents a very busy time for your agent, it is best not to concern your agent with anything more than a minor query and try to avoid being at the agency in person. The worst-case scenario is being resented for being in the way or leaving the agency with a sense of neglect.

Another point to consider is that although check-in is the most common time to be notified of work and castings, last-minute changes can occur throughout the day. Therefore, if you are informed that your chart is clear for the following day, then do not assume you will be free. This assumption can lead to you being unavailable without your agent's knowledge and they might propose you for a job or casting you cannot reach in time. If you are notified of a free day and wish to use the opportunity for personal matters, then you must always tell your agent of your unavailability. However, beware that you do not miss out on castings or bookings and, unless they are essential, personal errands are best left to the weekend.

Overall, the daily check-in system is designed to avoid any miscommunication between models, agents and, ultimately, clients, but nothing is set in stone, making the need to be available, or at least contactable, crucial.

BOOKING OUT

A major perk of working as a model is the flexibility of your schedule. If you decide to take time off, then as boss and business owner, it is always your decision whether to go to work or not. Of course, not working means not earning and holiday pay and sick leave are not privileges enjoyed by models. However, regardless of your work ethic, it is crucial to inform the agency if you decide to take some time off. This is known as booking out, and whether you are unavailable to work for just a morning dental appointment or for a two-week summer holiday, booking out well in advance will avoid your booker making promises to clients on your behalf that cannot be honoured. This is especially apparent if your need to book out is unavoidable.

I know a model who …

never checks in. In the end, she stopped getting proposed for jobs.

AVOIDING COSTLY SCAMS

There are many fantastic and genuine model agencies and being scouted by one can mean the start of an exciting chapter in your life. However, wherever there is a way of making money, there will always be a few people looking to exploit those hoping to break into the industry. These fake 'agents' rely heavily on the naivety and ambition of their targets, but by recognizing the warning signs you can avoid being conned.

Fake 'scouts' or 'spotters' will usually operate in public places such as shopping centres and high streets, gaining the attention of their intended victim with a mixture of flattery, lies and false promises. Quite often they use famous names as a distraction, before proposing their target spend money on professional photographs, registration fees or website costs.

If you are stopped in the street, there are ways you can ensure the legitimacy of a scout's or agency's claims. For example, in the UK, the Association of Model Agents (AMA) lists most the reputable agencies across the country on their website and because most mobile phones will let you access the Internet instantly, you can check legitimacy on the spot.

If you are unable to verify what the scout is telling you, then remember never to give out your personal details. After all, if an agency scout likes your look, they will show interest and leave the rest to you. Also, if they like you today, then they'll like you tomorrow, so never make snap decisions or feel pressured into signing anything. Instead, politely say that you'll think about it, before taking their details and walking away. As soon as you are home, research them online and if they claim to be from a high-profile agency, then phone the agency and check that the scout is affiliated with them.

Another red flag you should look out for is scouts promising a modelling contract, but only after some professional shots have been taken. Some con artists will charge exorbitant amounts of money for a few simple head shots, and so if a scout is proposing this, they are guaranteed to be misleading you. If anything, professional shots will hinder your chances of gaining representation because agencies want to see how you photograph in natural light and in your natural state. For this, all you need is a basic digital camera and a willing friend, partner or family member to press the button.

As well as operating on the high street, some scam artists often stalk their prey in cyberspace by using social networking sites, instant messenger programmes and chat rooms. Here, they pose as bookers from established agents and suggest the intended victim spends time and money building a portfolio with the promise of a modelling contract. However, reputable model agencies rarely contact prospective models via the Internet. If you are approached in this way, then always check the email address coincides with the agency website and phone the agency directly to verify any claims.

Occasionally a bogus agency can charge registration or administrative fees and claim this to be an industry standard, but once again these are lies. An agent will invest time and money in you because they believe they will recoup that money from the work you will acquire. If you are really unsure, then it is best not to proceed and seek out an alternative, legitimate agent for yourself.

LIFE AS A NEW FACE

Once you have an agent, you'll be sent out to meet clients, attend castings and test with various photographers. Knowing what to carry with you at all times will ensure you are prepared for anything.

MODEL MYTH MAKEOVER

'SIZE ZERO IS THE WAY TO GO'

Fact: anorexia and bulimia nervosa are very serious illnesses. A person suffering from an eating disorder will experience body dysmorphia, feelings of helplessness and constant thoughts about food. Frequently, the sufferer will engage in highly ritualistic behaviour as a way of feeling in control, as well as concealing their illness from those closest to them. Current psychological understanding is that both genetic and environmental factors cause the disease and, unfortunately, treatments offer few guarantees of recovery. The onset of anorexia and bulimia usually occur during adolescence, which is a turbulent period both socially and biochemically. It is also a time that many boys and, particularly, girls, consider entering the world of fashion. However, it is a common misconception that all models are stick thin and have eating disorders.

There are few rules about when a career begins and even fewer about when it should end.

Recent trends in the industry have actively veered away from the super-skinny towards a healthy physical ideal. In fact, one of the fastest growing areas in fashion is for plus-size models. The occasional high-profile story in the news and general obsession about body size in the media have not helped, but the truth is that the vast majority of working models have a normal relationship with their daily meals and approach their body image in much the same way as everyone else does.

Nevertheless, being judged on physical appearance does put extra strains on a person's self-esteem, and for those more susceptible to the effects of this pressure, the industry must consider its role in ensuring the health and well-being of the models it uses. The solution, as ever, is education; firstly, by educating models that a slim, healthy physique is attained by eating the right foods and not by avoiding food altogether. Educating agents and bookers that flippant remarks about a person's weight or body shape can have vast repercussions on their state of mind is also key. Finally, clients should be encouraged to use only girls who exude health and contentment.

If you notice changes in your fellow models or, more importantly, in yourself, then speak to someone immediately. We all have things we would like to change about our bodies, and with patience, a well-balanced diet and plenty of exercise and rest, we can. Furthermore, clever lighting, styling and make-up, digital photography and post-production can hide just about everything, so comparisons with magazines, television or the photographs in your own portfolio will not help.

PARTY SCENE PROMISES

One of the perks of being a model is getting the VIP treatment at some really glamorous events. Free entry to nightclubs, table service, free drinks, free model dinners, chauffeurs and access to exclusive parties are pretty standard and have led to an idea that models are hedonistic party animals caught in an industry awash with drug and alcohol abuse. The truth is that substance abuse is prevalent in all areas of our society regardless of age, sex or occupation and is an unfortunate side effect of a culture that prides itself on instant gratification, excess and escapism.

One way to avoid party scene promises is not to think that networking is essential in order to get ahead. This belief, that being 'seen' will assist their career, can put pressure on models to accept every invitation they receive. However, in order to be successful, you need to save your energy for when it matters: on castings and on jobs. Both alcohol and drug use are personal choices but one universal maxim is that your look, book and attitude will suffer from constant late nights, toxins and missing out on early morning castings.

Don't be tempted by club promoters who actively seek out attractive girls to accompany them to parties. Promises of whom you're likely to meet and opportunities to network are almost always exaggerated because it's their job. And remember: no one ever booked a campaign in a nightclub, because that type of decision is carefully made in the sober light of day and by a group of people.

Life in the big city is not for everyone and commuting is always an option.

RIGHT PLACE, WRONG TIME

A common mistake that people make is that a career in modelling is a very short one. They believe that girls and boys start in their teens and have perhaps five to ten years to make it before moving on. In reality, there are no hard and fast rules about when to start or when to retire as a model. As long as you maintain a good look, book and attitude and find clients who are willing to confirm you for work, your age shouldn't matter. Instead, as a model ages, they simply shift their client base accordingly, and, if they so choose, a model's career can span decades. In fact, the majority of the bigger money clients prefer to use models with a little more gravitas because of their perceived confidence, self-assuredness and ability to connect with the consumer. Furthermore, there are even some jobs that legally require models of a certain age.

Whilst it is true that modelling success is not instantaneous, and the lifestyle is perhaps suited to younger boys and girls with fewer commitments, each career path is unique, meaning you're never to old too start and certainly never too old continue. If you are a little older and considering starting, then your choice of agency is very important. Research the agencies online and look for a 'best age' or 'classics' division that deals with more mature models.

LOCATION, LOCATION, LOCATION

There are boys and girls with the potential to model all over the globe and yet the main focus of the industry appears to be just in a select few cities. London, New York, Paris and Milan seem to have all the main fashion houses, leading some to believe that in order to be a success, a model must live and work in one of these cities. In truth, there are markets all over the world and with digital photography and the Internet, geography is not a restriction. Whilst clients tend to converge towards larger cities, there is always work to be found in smaller markets and it can be a great way to develop before heading to a big city.

If the idea of living in the city doesn't appeal, then remember that modelling is not a typical nine-to-five job and commuting is a common alternative for both new faces and established models. Most public transport systems into major cities allow fast and easy access to a host of desirable clients and by going home to friends and family, you can maintain a distinct boundary between your professional and personal life. If you're really unsure, then start by researching local model agencies and see if you'd like to go further. (However, be careful with scam agencies who prefer to operate in smaller markets.) From there, investigate potential travel costs and compare them to the living costs of moving into the city. Above all, bear in mind that where you live should not stand in your way.

IN THE CLOSET

Traditionally, the fashion industry has been very tolerant and progressive in its view towards homosexuality, bisexuality and trans-genderism and this open-mindedness has meant that those in the business have never felt the need to conceal who they truly are. Perhaps this has given society grounds for assumption, but as with most stereotypes, the view that all male models, fashion designers and photographers are gay is way off the mark. After all, a person's sexual orientation is entirely their own business and has no bearing on the choices they make professionally. Homophobia has no place in modelling or in our society as a whole. With this, and indeed all the myths about our industry, it is the responsibility of all models to educate the wider population about what really goes on.

Final Thoughts on . . . New Faces

The difference between the girls today and models of the past is that now we are not only interested in fashion: we are going in so many different directions at once. We work harder – at night and on weekends.

Claudia Schiffer

In summary, by now you should have a good understanding of the way the industry works and how best to get your foot in the door. Once you have assessed your credentials and found an agency you are happy with, you can finally embark on your journey towards modelling success. However, don't be fooled into thinking that you are a fully-fledged model just because you have representation. Like any business, the first few months will be the hardest and will require a significant investment of both your time and money before you can enjoy the rewards. With focus and by synchronizing your look, book and attitude, you can quickly obtain a list of clients.

2: Your Look

Even I don't wake up looking like Cindy Crawford.

Cindy Crawford

The next two chapters focus on what people see when you walk into a room. As a professional model, your look is now a key factor in how much you can potentially earn and the more you maintain this look, the more visually appealing you will become. A toned physique, clear complexion and healthy hair all broadcast a positive message, as well as boost your own levels of confidence. Furthermore, by incorporating a clothing style that complements your personality and using the right make-up techniques to highlight your natural beauty, you can raise your self-esteem even further.

NUTRITION

It is no secret that a healthy, well-hydrated diet consisting of the required proteins, carbohydrates, fats, vitamins and minerals can significantly improve a person's physical appearance, energy levels, immune system and metabolism. However, whilst nutrients serve as fuel for the body, the role a meal plays in a person's life is so much more than this and food is as crucial to a person's psychological health as the constituent parts of a meal are for physical well-being. Furthermore, each person has a unique body and mind that need feeding in different ways. Whilst meal plans can help, it is up to the individual to take the time to listen to the language their body is speaking and translate what is being said. In doing so, you can develop a healthy relationship with your breakfast, lunch and dinner and soon realize that healthy eating should be celebrated and not feared. Also, a balanced diet allows you to confidently indulge in the more pleasurable, but perhaps less functional, meals from time to time.

With so many contradictions about the correct combination of nutrients, ideal portion size and meal times, identifying and then implementing a healthy diet can be difficult. The best place to start is with the crucial distinction between 'being on a diet' and 'having a good diet'. In recent times fad diets have been touted as the easiest way to a trim figure, but, basically, they all 'work' by encouraging a blanket restriction of nutrients, regardless of their value, and do not take into consideration either the dieter's activity levels or personal metabolism. This self-imposed starvation is really unhealthy and neither sustainable for more than a few days, nor effective in the long term. Worse still, starving the body is dangerous and, in extreme circumstances, can be fatal.

The reason restrictive diets don't work is because the sudden lack of nutrition serves only to slow the body's metabolic rate. This is the speed at which the body processes nutrients, produces energy and clears waste. Whilst there are genetic factors in how fast the system functions, the way you treat your metabolism directly affects your quality of life in return. Significantly less energy, a dip in immunity levels, problems with digestion and a disruption of sleeping patterns all result from severely restricting food intake. Even more counter-productive are the hormones triggered in response to a bout of starvation. These signal the body to actually store more fat, and any weight lost during dieting is almost immediately regained as the dieter not only slips back into bad eating habits, but also as their body prepares for future food deprivation. Overall, people on extremely low-calorie diets are often tired, stressed and unwell.

Instead, nutritionists agree that having a balanced diet is a consistent and sustainable solution not only for long-term health, but also for visible results. Therefore, devising a meal plan tailored to your physical needs and personal tastes is the best place to start. As a model, your daily routine can be extremely varied: an early call time one day and a night shoot the next. Education about the constituent parts of any meal can help, but in order to create a plan that is flexible and robust enough to function in the real world, you need to go one step further and embrace a daily lifestyle that is sustained by healthy eating. This doesn't mean you should become obsessive about the food you put into your system, but remember to listen your body and respond accordingly. The messages your body sends to you about how effectively a food type is digested and utilized are just as clear as the messages about its taste and texture. You just need to tune into what you are being told by experimenting and cutting out all the unnecessary or unhealthy parts of your diet.

One example is lactose, which is a sugar predominantly found in milk and other dairy products. Research suggests that most people are unable to properly digest lactose, which leads to the immune system treating the sugar molecules in the same way as an invading bacteria. The symptoms of lactose intolerance can range from mild bloating and a dip in energy to severe stomach cramps and diarrhoea. However, until a person cuts lactose out of their diet, they will not realize that life need not be a constant struggle against fatigue and digestive

I always wear what I'm comfortable in. If one designer doesn't like what I'm wearing, the next one will.

Coco Rocha

problems. Wheat and gluten are also problematic, but prevalent in many people's diets. Try cutting various food types like bread, pasta and dairy products out of your diet and analyse the way you feel. Then, reintroduce them one at a time and study the effects. You may be surprised at what you find.

A few other areas that are also important are portion size, meal times and dietary supplements. People will often severely restrict the size of their meals, stop eating food after a certain point in the day and rely on pills as a substitute for food. Furthermore, they rigidly adhere to these restrictions regardless of what they are doing or how they feel. Employ common sense, and with portion size, for example, eat slowly enough for the body to tell the brain when it is sated. Then, when you feel full, simply stop eating. Over time you'll be able to accurately judge your required portion size during meal preparation.

What time you eat your meals also requires a little thought, but remember that a bad calorie is a bad calorie regardless of the time of day it is eaten. The effects of eating unhealthy food are just as detrimental in the morning as they are in the evening. On the other hand, going to bed whilst extremely hungry is stressful and likely to lead to a broken night's sleep. Fatigue increases the likelihood of you craving sugary treats and overeating during meals. Also, if you are vigorously active late in the day, you have to replenish the nutrients lost whilst exercising, so a good meal close to bedtime can aid rest, recovery and repair.

In addition, some argue a well-balanced diet shouldn't need supplementing and that the dietary supplement business has become a multi-million dollar industry by using a mixture of clever marketing and lazy consumerism to sell tablets and tinctures by the ton. Retailers claim to boost body function or cure ailments with a simple daily dose, but in reality many supplements are nothing more than placebos. Vitamins and minerals are abundant in nature and by ensuring your meals are colourful and varied, you can save money and get the same results.

Overall, education, preparation and flexibility are key. You should eat when you hungry and stop when you are full. If you have a craving for a particular meal, there may be nutrients within that food you are lacking. The Model Meal Plan is a useful guide, but once you build on this basic knowledge, you can adapt it in any way you choose.

PROTEIN

Proteins consist of long chains of amino acids that are linked by peptides. When digested, these links are broken, allowing the body to reconfigure the amino acids into new chains for growth, repair and virtually all biological processes. There are about twenty different types of amino acid and a typical protein may contain combinations of 500 or more. The body can make certain amino acids, but there are also some that it cannot make itself. These are known as essential amino acids and have to be obtained from a person's diet. They include: leucine, isoleucine, valine, threonine, methionine, phenylalanine, tryptophan, and lysine. Furthermore, the body can't store protein, making it a daily requirement in any well-balanced diet. In fact, every meal should include at least some protein.

There remains debate over the best sources of dietary protein not only in terms of their quality, but other factors as well, including their digestibility and associated nutritional value. Animal proteins are complete

The yolk and albumen combine to form a perfect protein powerhouse.

Include protein in every main meal.

proteins whilst vegetable proteins are not. Therefore, some consider a vegetarian diet, for example, to be protein-deficient. However, meat is also higher in fat and cholesterol and so the added amino acids may come at

a cost. Similarly, cheese contains whey, a complete protein, but for those who are allergic to dairy products, this may be an unusable source.

Fortunately, the fact that most foods contain at least some protein means that with enough variation, whatever your tastes, morals, budget or religion, dietary protein will never be in short supply. Good sources include red meat, poultry, fish, nuts and seeds, pulses, soya products, cereals such as oats and rice, eggs, milk, cheese and yoghurt. A useful technique to ensure enough dietary protein has been acquired and that you are not restricted to one type is to rotate your daily source. For example, Monday could be a vegetarian day, Tuesday chicken, Wednesday fish, and so on.

CARBOHYDRATES

All carbohydrates consist of chains of different sugar molecules that group together in varying lengths and in different ways. The most basic chains are 'simple' carbohydrates. For example, the simple carbohydrate sucrose, or table sugar as it is more commonly known, consists of just one fructose molecule and one glucose molecule. However, as these sugar chains increase in length and intricacy, they become 'complex' carbohydrates.

Salmon is full of essential proteins and fatty acids.

A bowl of porridge in the morning will keep you active for hours.

Starches are an example of more complex carbohydrates and can have hundreds of long, branching molecules, all linked together.

Once in the digestive system, the complexity of the carbohydrate determines the speed at which it is broken down and absorbed into the blood stream. The more complex the carbohydrate, the slower the sugar release,

Quick to eat but slow to release carbohydrates. Plus, bananas are full of potassium.

I know a model who ...

always raids the chocolate in the fridge of photo studios. She gets through three or four bars in a day!

Sweet potatoes: baked, mashed, boiled or roasted – just as versatile as white potatoes, but with a much lower GI.

A few examples of food types and their associated glycaemic index (GI)	
Food type (150g serving)	GI
Glucose	100
Steamed white rice	98
Baguette	95
Jacket potato	85
Rice cakes	82
French fries	75
Bran flakes	74
White bread	70
Wholemeal bread	69
Fresh pineapple	66
Rye bread	65
Couscous	65
Basmati rice	58
Honey	58
Banana	55
Quinoa	53
Kiwi fruit	52
Baked beans in tomato sauce	48
Orange juice	46
Lentil soup	44
Chickpeas, canned	42
Apples	38
Wholemeal spaghetti	37
Skimmed milk	32
Dried apricot	30
Whole milk	27
Grapefruit	25
Barley	22
Soy milk	17
Low-fat yoghurt	14
Hummus	6

and if absorption occurs all at once, a spike in blood sugar levels occurs, triggering mechanisms that convert any excess sugar into fat for storage and later use.

The most effective way to distinguish simple from complex carbohydrates is by paying attention to the glycaemic index (GI) of the food. This is calculated by observing the direct effect that the food has on blood sugar and then assigning it a number between one and a hundred. For normal daily activities, the lower the glycaemic index of a food, the more beneficial it is. Try to avoid foods with a high GI unless directly after vigorous sporting activities, and even then only have controlled amounts. Refined carbohydrates, such as sugar, white flour and alcohol (which is one of the sources with the highest number of simple carbohydrates) are not recommended as over time these can cause health complications such as diabetes. The GI table below should help you to distinguish which carbohydrates you should incorporate into your daily diet.

FAT

In today's society, and particularly within the fashion industry, the word 'fat' seems to have negative conno-

I eat like a horse!

Elle Macpherson

Avocados can be sliced, spread or even blended to make a healthy condiments.

Have nuts as a snack or add a handful to a main meal.

Not all olive oils are the same. Some are better for cooking with, whilst others are best suited to salad dressing.

tations, and people think it is something that should be avoided at all costs. However, whilst there are undeniably harmful fats, there are also a wide variety of essential fatty acids, lipids and oils that are crucial for health and can significantly improve the body's metabolism. In fact, the digestion, absorption and transportation of certain vitamins responsible for healthy vision, immunity from disease, liver function and general well-being cannot occur without a good supply of dietary fat. The secret is to distinguish between the harmful and beneficial fats, and adjust your diet accordingly.

The most well-known distinctions within the fat family are between unsaturated and saturated fats. Without getting too scientific, these terms refer to the number of double bonds between the carbon atoms within the compound. This, in turn, affects the way the body can metabolize the fat and whether it is utilized or stored. Unsaturated fats have a high number of double bonds, meaning that when they are being broken down, less energy – or fewer calories – are released. There are three types of unsaturated fat: monounsaturated fats, polyunsaturated fats and essential fatty acids, like omega-3, omega-6 and omega-9. All are better than saturates at assisting metabolic function without producing excess energy. Furthermore, essential fatty acids cannot be synthesized by the body and must be acquired from a person's diet. Examples of unsaturated fats can be found in oily fish, eggs, cashew nuts, avocados, flax seed, olive oil and even kiwi fruit. Moderation is still encouraged, as there are links between excessive consumption of unsaturated fats and health problems.

Saturated fats, like those found in meat and dairy products, have fewer double bonds and therefore a higher calorific content. Whilst they are still important for a balanced diet, saturates have been repeatedly linked to cancers of the digestive tract, complications in heart function and higher cholesterol levels. Try to manage the amount of saturated fats in your food by reducing your red meat intake and cutting back on cheese and butter.

One type of fat that is particularly harmful, yet widespread in society, is the hydrogenated trans-fatty acid, or trans-fat as it is more commonly referred to. This type of fat rarely occurs in nature and is manufactured by breaking the double bonds of a polyunsaturate to create a saturate. This increases its resistance to rancidity and is, therefore, ideal for restaurants or processed food manufacturers interested in extending the life of their product. However, trans-fats are now considered so detrimental to a person's health that in the last few years there have been calls to completely ban their use in the food industry. An increasing body of evidence now links trans-fats to everything from a higher chance of coronary diseases, to a hindrance of learning and memory. Thus, most nutritionists recommend the only genuinely safe level of dietary hydrogenated fat is zero. Take-away food, chocolate bars, crisps, certain breads and baked goods, as well as ready meals, are all likely to contain trans-fats. There are plenty of alternatives for snacks like fruit, nuts, carrot sticks and hummus. Even at times when you which to indulge, higher-quality cakes and chocolate need not contain trans-fats.

FIBRE

Fibre is an indigestible material that not only assists digestion, but also slows the breakdown and absorption of carbohydrates, reducing their effect on blood sugar.

Brown rice is one of the best examples of a fibre that helps digestion and slows the absorption of carbohydrates.

Many people suffer from an intolerance to wheat but are unaware of this. Switch to rye bread and gauge your energy levels and digestive sensation. You might be pleasantly surprised.

The main sources of dietary fibre are fruits, vegetables and cereals and although it is now commonplace to see the 'five portions of fruit and veg a day' notices on packaging and in supermarkets, this is considered a minimum. Thankfully, considering one portion is only 100 grams (3.5 ounces), and a regular orange or banana will take care of two portions, having enough fibre in your diet should not be daunting or unattainable. However, it must be noted that whilst frozen fruit and vegetables are just as beneficial as fresh ones, the same cannot be said for dried fruits, processed fruit juices and yoghurt containing fruit.

VITAMINS AND MINERALS

Vitamins and minerals can be found everywhere and yet it is easy to miss out on several key ones by not having a varied diet. Below is a table highlighting how the body uses various vitamins and where they can be found.

Good news for vegetarians. Chickpeas are full of fibre and, when combined with green vegetables, make a complete protein.

Spinach is a 'super food' and is full of antioxidants.

Vitamins: their uses and sources

Vitamins	Uses	Examples of dietary sources
Vitamin A (retinol)	Promotes healthy vision and growth and repair	Carrot, mango, sweet potato, pumpkin, tomato
Vitamin B1 (thiamin)	Nerve function and metabolism	Soy, pork, spinach
Vitamin B2 (riboflavin)	Vision and skin	Mushroom, eggs, broccoli, liver
Vitamin B3 (niacin)	Digestion and nerve function	Spinach, chicken, tuna
Vitamin B6 (pyridoxine)	Red blood cell production and fatty acid metabolism	Bananas, spinach, chicken breast
Vitamin B12	Cell reproduction	Meat, poultry, eggs, fish
Vitamin C	Immunity, amino acid metabolism, iron absorption	Spinach, broccoli, strawberries, mango, kiwi fruit, orange
Vitamin D	Bone mineralization	Egg yolk, oily fish, UV sunlight
Vitamin E	Skin cell regeneration and anti-oxidization	Avocado, quinoa, brown rice, polyunsaturated oils
Vitamin K	Healing	Leafy green vegetables

Minerals: their uses and sources

Minerals	Uses	Examples of dietary sources
Calcium	Strengthen teeth and bones	Milk, spinach, broccoli, tofu
Chloride	Digestion and electrolyte balance	Eggs, meat, salt
Chromium	Energy release and insulin production	Olive oil, cheese, nuts
Copper	Enzyme production, the absorption of iron and blood cell formation	Meat, water
Fluoride	Tooth decay resistance	Tea, seafood
Iodine	Metabolic rate maintenance, growth and repair	Wholegrains, milk, cheese, seafood
Iron	Essential for haemoglobin which is found in red blood cells	Meat, tomato, spinach, artichoke, parsley, broccoli, shrimp
Magnesium	Growth and muscle repair and essential for the nervous system	Black-eyed peas, sunflower seeds, cashew nuts, halibut
Molybdenum	Cellular activity	Meat, legumes
Potassium	Muscle contractions and maintaining electrolyte balance	Banana, avocado, cod, spinach, carrot, strawberries, watermelon
Phosphorus	Development of bones and teeth	Meat, fish, poultry, eggs
Selenium	Antioxidant good for skin, nails and hair	Seafood, Brazil nuts, quinoa
Sodium	Nerve transmission and electrolyte balance	Seafood, soy sauce, milk, meat, cheese
Zinc	Protein synthesis, growth and repair and sperm production	Ham, oysters, lentils, beef, spinach, broccoli, green peas

Tomatoes are full of lycopene, which helps fight cancer, cardiovascular disease and diabetes.

Broccoli is one of the best sources of vitamin C, which is essential for your immune system.

WATER

Water is essential for us to stay alive and whilst a person can live for weeks with little or no food, dehydration kills in just a few days. As extreme as this example is, it highlights the importance of staying well hydrated. Water is

Blueberries improve vision and mental function and have been linked to reducing fat around the waist.

I don't like to wear anything too tight because I need to feel I can eat. Food is the most important thing to me.

Helena Christensen

If you're thirsty, you may already be dehydrated because your body needs a constant supply of water to function efficiently.

Apples are over 80 per cent water.

Eating healthily means learning how to cook. You don't have to be a cordon bleu chef, but the more meals you prepare for yourself, the more control you will have over what goes into your body.

important for everything from higher energy levels to a clearer complexion and whilst scientists recommend that we drink at least two litres of fluid a day, it is easier to listen to what your body is telling you. As with food, learning the body's language will benefit you, and sometimes you may think you're hungry or tired, but actually your body is telling you that it is dehydrated. Experiment by grabbing a glass of water the next time you feel this way, wait a few minutes and see if the hunger or fatigue have passed. The human body is over 60 per cent water, so remember: the wetter, the better.

THE MODEL MEAL PLAN

The following suggested weekly meal plan is a rough guide to what a balanced diet should be. Use it as a starting point and if you wish to tailor the meals, rotation days, quantities and frequencies to suit your personal lifestyle, then feel free to do so. Remember: as a model, your schedule will change from week to week, so prepare meals in advance of when you know you'll be out and about. Anticipating hunger reduces the likelihood of having to buy expensive or processed convenience foods.

Preparation for your meal plan begins at the supermarket, and as a model, you should use your flexible schedule to visit the supermarket several times a week. Always buy fresh, frozen or unprocessed produce and avoid grocery shopping when you are hungry, as you are more likely succumb to impulse buys. Once the food is in your kitchen, try to anticipate when you will be hungry and prepare a meal accordingly. This stifles extreme hunger and subsequent overeating.

I know a model who ...

yo-yo diets so much that she never looks like the photos on her card. It always causes friction on shoots.

The Model Meal Plan

	Monday	Tuesday	Wednesday	Thursday	Friday	Saturday	Sunday
Rotation Day	Vegetarian day	Chicken day	Fish day	Red meat day	Vegetarian day	Fish day	Chicken day
	Water	Water	Water	Water	Water	Water	Water
Breakfast	Gluten-free porridge with lactose-free milk and honey	Spinach and tomato omelette	Mackerel over avocado spread on rye bread	Poached eggs with organic ham and grilled peppers	Gluten-free porridge with lactose-free milk and honey	Mixed nuts, seeds and berries with natural yoghurt	Lactose-free milk mixed berry smoothie
	Water	Water	Water	Water	Water	Water	Water
Snack	Freshly made carrot, orange and ginger juice	Lactose-free milk banana smoothie	Apple and brie	Lactose-free milk banana smoothie	Assorted fruit	Freshly made carrot, orange and ginger juice	Chicken liver pate with rye crackers and cucumber
	Water	Water	Water	Water	Water	Water	Water
Lunch	Tomato, beetroot, goat's cheese and avocado on rye bread	Home-made chicken salad wrap with hummus	Green vegetable and quinoa salad	Stir-fried vegetables, cashew nuts and quinoa	Chickpea curry with brown rice	Tuna salad with olive oil, coarse grain mustard and lemon juice	Roast chicken, cherry tomatoes and garlic with baked sweet potato and peas
Snack	Raw garden peas	Mixed nuts and seeds	Carrot and celery with hummus	Mixed nuts and seeds	Carrot and celery with hummus	Raw garden peas	Assorted fruit
	Water	Water	Water	Water	Water	Water	Water
Dinner	Chickpea salad with olive oil, coarse grain mustard and lemon juice	Home-made lentil soup	Smoked salmon salad with olive oil, coarse grain mustard and lemon juice	Fillet steak with steamed broccoli and spinach, and grilled tomato	Home-made carrot, ginger and goat's cheese soup	Baked fillet of salmon with steamed broccoli and spinach	Boiled eggs with asparagus

Top nutrition tips!

- Fats burn fat. Quality polyunsaturates are essential for a high metabolic rate, so go nuts.

- No such thing as a bad egg. They are quick and easy, provide great protein and the effects on cholesterol in the bloodstream have been exaggerated in the media.

- Grab a glass of water as soon as you wake up – it will kick-start your day. And remember: fluids can be gleaned from fruit, vegetables and smoothies as well as water.

- Fancy some chocolate? Here's the trick – have some dark chocolate with at least 70 per cent cocoa after a workout when blood sugar is low. It will also boost your serotonin levels.

- Home-made soups are a great way to get nutrients and be hydrated simultaneously. Experiment with different ingredients and consistencies.

- You should eat 1.5g (0.053oz) of protein a day for every kilo (2.25lb) you weigh.

- Go old school and bin the microwave. Microwaving food not only reduces its nutritional value, but also makes it harder to digest. Take your time and cook food.

- Steam your greens to retain their nutrients and grill your meat to remove excess fats.

- A good night's rest prevents overeating. Tiredness unbalances your hormones and you're more likely to reach for simple carbohydrates as your body struggles to wake up.

- Use colour as an indicator of nutritional variety. The more colourful your meals are, the better.

I know a model who ...

starves herself all day because she's so worried about her weight. She has to go to bed at eight o'clock because she is so tired. Also, when she does eat, it's always chocolate and crisps because her body is obviously craving sugar.

The changes you bring into your diet are designed to improve your physical appearance, energy levels and metabolism. However, if you are not enjoying the experience or certain aspects of the Model Meal Plan aren't working for you, then adapt it as you see fit. At the beginning, try introducing small changes that are not too pervasive or sudden. For example, start by switching your daily fizzy drink to an extra glass of water. As well as the additional hydration, this will result in 50,000 fewer calories over the course of a year. Thus, it's clear that a very small change on a daily basis can have a massive effect over time.

Above all, whilst nutrition can be viewed as a science, it is crucial to remember that balance is the key. Expression through cooking, the many different social occasions associated with food and the overall experience of eating are just as relevant as the metabolic processes. The psychological benefits from letting your hair down and enjoying yourself once in a while will also reflect positively on your relationships, your career and, most importantly, your life.

The secret is to listen to your body, eat healthily, exercise regularly and rest well. Your significantly higher metabolic rate will grant you the added bonus of being better suited to absorb the occasional indulgence. That is why there should be no such thing as a 'guilty pleasure', because if you respect your body's needs, your mind can relax about the odd snack.

Equally, malnutrition results in a decreased metabolic rate and manifests itself as less available energy and a greater chance of health and mental problems. The positive effects of healthy eating improve personal appearance, and loss of fat, improved muscle growth and clear, healthy skin soon become apparent. Eat right, look good. Simple.

The Model Meal Plan should act as a rough guide and starting point for a healthy diet. Adapt it, improve it and, most importantly, personalize it.

Overall, between the Model Meal Plan and the information provided, you now have enough knowledge to improve your diet. Try your best to cut out refined sugars and hydrogenated fats, and reduce your saturated fat and alcohol consumption. Remember: eating well requires effort, and more specifically anticipation and preparation. Without application, education is useless.

Stay hydrated when you exercise or your performance will be severely impaired.

EXERCISE

Having a good body is essential for being a successful commercial model. A toned physique will look better in photographs and on the catwalk, and will give you the confidence to shine in situations most people would shy away from. However, results cannot be achieved without a great deal of sweat, hard work and exercise. The good news is that the list of benefits of challenging your body on a regular basis are almost endless: increased energy levels, more restful nights, an improvement in mental ability, better blood circulation, a clearer complexion, an improved digestive system and a reduction in the chances of everything from osteoporosis to breast cancer. Also, research has shown that looking after your body leads to increased dopamine levels, making healthy people also happy people. Better still, the effects of this mental boost are almost instantaneous.

With all these benefits, you might be tempted to dust off your trainers and head straight to the gym, but with so many contrasting views about the best way to exercise, knowing where to start can be confusing. Therefore, in order to cut through all the nonsense, you simply need to understand the language your body speaks and then ensure you listen to it every time you exercise. Thankfully, you don't need a PhD in sport science to translate the messages your body sends you and devising a structured yet flexible routine will help you achieve noticeable changes to your body shape and enjoy the experience to boot.

DEVELOPING A ROUTINE

When developing an exercise plan, remember that it is your body and, therefore, your responsibility to understand the way it works. Most gyms provide complimentary fitness sessions with instructors and personal trainers, and health and fitness magazines offer advice and specific exercises designed to pinpoint certain areas. However, it is much better to take control of your training by devising your own balanced routine. Here, the word 'balance' has many different interpretations and they are all equally important.

Everyone – men and women – should always incorporate postural exercises and stretching into daily life to prevent muscular and skeletal imbalances. Also, performing regular core exercises ensures a balanced spine as well as harmony between the unseen inner muscles and more visible outer ones. Furthermore, you need to find a balance between anaerobic and aerobic exercise to ensure your nervous, muscular and cardiovascular systems all get a complete workout.

During resistance training, again balance is key, and

by including a variety of movements into your workout, you can burn fat and build muscle in a more efficient way. Just as crucial as the training is employing a healthy balance between exercise and rest, allowing your body and mind time to recover from regular exertion. In addition, remember that your body cannot perform well without a healthy and balanced diet and that even if your goal is to lose weight, you shouldn't test your body's limits without the correct nutrients.

Overall, the body is such a complex system that imbalances will not only slow your progress, but will actually cause regression if not addressed. Remember to mix up your routine on a weekly or monthly basis to keep your exercise regime fun and fresh. If going to the gym doesn't appeal to you, or your travels take you away from home, there are many different activities you can engage in, both indoors and out, that will still keep you in shape. Resistance training using your own body weight, running, boxing, rowing, yoga, Pilates, swimming, climbing or taking dance classes are all ways to burn calories, improve muscle tone and increase heart function. Better still, mix up your routine and try new and different activities each week so that your body is always being challenged in slightly different ways.

POSTURE

Having a good posture is not only crucial for your look as a model but also extremely important for skeletal and muscular development. In fact, without the correct posture and technique during exercise, the chances of short-term injury and long-term complications are greatly increased. For example, something as simple as jogging can cause spinal problems if there is an undetected postural issue. Over the course of months and years, if untreated, the problem perpetuates itself until the sufferer can no longer run without experiencing debilitating pain and displaying one or more visual abnormalities. Therefore, ensuring a technique that strengthens your posture and offers your spine maximum support is key. Better still, before you lift your first weight or attend your first class, assess your posture and treat it accordingly.

There are many different postural problems and it is best to seek a professional assessment of your skeleton's alignment, as well as the shape of your spine, before you can proceed with a serious routine. The most common postural problems, however, all stem from repeated behaviours that cause to muscle imbalances. If not corrected, these can lead to excessive curving of the spine at different points. For example, carrying your portfolio in a satchel over the same shoulder can lead to scoliosis, which is a lopsided posture. Therefore, you should keep your portfolio in a rucksack that evenly distributes the weight across both shoulders.

Below are examples of muscle imbalances that have resulted in bad postures. If you recognize any of these signs in your own posture, you should aim to correct them immediately and before progressing onto a rigorous exercise routine.

Rounded Shoulders
Rounded shoulders are usually combated by stretching the chest, latissimus dorsi and abdominal muscles, whilst

Rounded shoulders don't look good in photographs.

An excessively curved lumbar spine can cause severe back pain if not treated.

Scoliosis is very common and is usually the result of carrying a bag on the same side since childhood.

increasing the strength of the muscles between the shoulder blades, known as the rhomboids and lower trapezius. Also, stretching and strengthening the rotator cuff muscles and training the posterior deltoids will help.

Excessively Curved Lumbar Spine

An excessively curved lumbar spine is most commonly dealt with by stretching the hip flexors and hamstrings. Core work will significantly improve this problem area, particularly lower abdominal exercises.

Scoliosis

The lower shoulder line is caused by tension drawing the muscles down, and correcting a lopsided posture is therefore simply a case of stretching these muscles whilst strengthening the opposite side. As with all postural imbalances, erroneous daily behaviour will

undo your hard work, so be sure not to exacerbate the problem.

As well as postural exercises, a fundamental way to establish muscular balance is by strengthening inner core muscles to support your spine.

CORE

When considering how best to train your core, it is crucial to understand the difference between the inner and outer core muscles. The inner core consists of muscle tissue dedicated to protecting the body's vital organs around the midriff and bridging the skeletal gap between the ribs and pelvis. The stronger and more robust this complex group of muscles are, the more balance, strength and support a person will have when training other muscles including the outer core and limbs. Therefore, before attempting to develop the

Core 1: Focus on an even distribution of weight and a relaxed but controlled spine. Minimal movements can have a significant effects, especially for those just starting out. If it's too easy, then move on to more advanced techniques.

Progression A: Remember to only raise your hand and knee just a fraction. It will promote better balance and control.

abdominal muscles with exercises like sit-ups, it is vital to engage and strengthen the inner core. Without this foundation, movements designed to improve abdominal strength could result in short-term injury and long-term muscle imbalance.

There are many basic core exercises that are often overlooked, even by experienced gym-goers. Below is the best example of how to strengthen your core and two progressions that can be incorporated as the muscles develop. Perform these towards end of your workout, at least four times a week. However, if you suffer from postural problems or if abdominal exercising results in back and neck pain, then make these core exercises your priority. Better still, do them as soon as you wake every morning. It is a great way to strengthen your core and the deep breathing aids metabolic and mental state.

Core Exercise One

START POSITION
Start on all fours with your hands and knees directly below your shoulders and hips, respectively. Your face should be directed towards the floor, your weight evenly distributed across all four limbs and your spine should be

in a neutral position. 'Neutral' means running straight with neither your upper nor lower back curving excessively.

ACTION
From here, inhale slowly over six to eight seconds and as the oxygen fills your lungs, slowly drive your abdomen towards the floor. It is essential not to arch your back or move your spine in any way whatsoever. Hold the air before slowly exhaling and simultaneously draw your navel towards your spine. Again, ensure a neutral spine and be sure to focus solely on your core muscles. Repeat this process ten times and then rest for one minute. Repeat the set a second and third time, each with a minute's rest in between. Once you can comfortably complete the entire exercise without undue fatigue or discomfort, it is time to move on to Progression A.

Progression A
Start in the same position as Core Exercise One. Remember to focus on your breathing and maintaining a neutral spine. Once again, inhale, forcing your abdomen towards the ground, but on the exhale, fractionally raise your left hand and right knee off the floor by no more than one centimetre or half an inch. Focus on bringing your navel towards your spine and maintaining the correct posture at all times. Hold the hand and knee off the floor for ten seconds, return to your

Progression B: If, during this exercise, you feel any undue stress in your lower back, then stop immediately and return to Core Exercise One and Progression A.

neutral position and repeat with the opposing limbs. Each set consists of ten raises on each side, and there are three sets in the entire exercise with a one-minute rest between the sets. Once you have mastered this exercise, move on to Progression B.

Progression B

Start in the same position as Core Exercise One. Inhale, force your navel towards the floor and briefly hold. Then, on the exhale, raise your left arm out in front of you, parallel to the floor and at a 45 degree angle to your

Progression B: Starting the exercise with a pole running the length of your body can really help your alignment. Try this at home with a broom handle, for example.

head. Meanwhile, simultaneously extend your right leg out behind you. Therefore, your final position is with both arm and leg extended in a line and parallel to the floor. Hold for ten seconds and during this time, focus on maintaining balance and ensure your navel is drawn towards your spine. Return to the neutral start position and then employ the same technique with the opposing limbs. Raise each arm and leg ten times to complete a set, perform three sets and have a one-minute rest in between.

Once you are at a stage where you can perform Core Exercise One and both Progression A and B, complete all three exercises consecutively. This should take fifteen to twenty minutes and, with regular training, will strengthen your core in a matter of weeks.

STRETCHING

There are many conflicting theories about stretching. Some argue that you should always stretch before training, but some findings suggest this doesn't reduce the chance of injury. Others insist post-workout stretching is more beneficial. One thing that is agreed

Yoga is a great way to breathe, relax and stretch at the same time.

is that good stretching requires time, energy and focus.

Dedicate at least fifteen to twenty minutes to your stretch routine and at a time when the body is well rested. Also, instead of stretching every muscle group regardless of flexibility, listen to your body, concentrating on the tighter areas to ensure a better equilibrium. Overstretching is not advised as it can reduce a muscle's functionality.

If you feel sharp pain then ease off or stop completely. As well as causing muscle and ligament damage, over-stretching can be detrimental to the nervous system. Beginner yoga classes are a great place to stretch in a relaxed and controlled environment.

*   *   *

Once you have the foundations of a good posture, a strong core and a level of flexibility that won't impede your development, you can confidently personalize your exercise routine in a way that will help you achieve your goals. However, regardless of what you are hoping to achieve from your training, it is essential to employ a healthy balance between anaerobic and aerobic exercise.

ANAEROBIC EXERCISE

The terms anaerobic and aerobic refer to the different ways in which the body produces energy. Basically, anaerobic exercise involves short bursts of high-intensity activity designed to recruit muscle and enhance power and strength. However, it is a bit of a misconception that anaerobic exercises such as weightlifting always result in big muscles and are only for boys who want to bulk up. Examples include resistance training, sprinting and swimming. The type and frequency of training, nutritional intake and natural hormone levels all affect muscle growth. In fact, muscle is quite an energy-expensive commodity, making it hard to maintain. Building lean muscle mass requires dedication and certainly won't happen after one or two weight sessions in the gym.

Resistance training is especially important for models hoping for a toned aesthetic. This leads to a second misconception, which is that muscle tone is achieved with light weights and high repetitions. This is incorrect because muscles grow with use or atrophy from in-activity. Thus it is impossible to shape your muscles in any particular direction and in order to attain a more 'toned' look and increase definition, you should employ a high level of intensity to burn off fat whilst building the muscle below.

When engaging in resistance training it is vital to incorporate various movements into your weekly training routine in order to ensure balanced muscular development. These movements are: squatting, lunging, lifting, pushing, pulling and rotating. Each motion has different 'prime movers', which are the muscles that activate and control the movement. If you perform these exercises and find they are not working your prime movers, then your technique may be incorrect or you may have muscular imbalances that need addressing.

Squat

Ensure your feet are facing forward and just wider than hip-width apart. Soft knees and a neutral alignment of

Finish position for a squat. Examples include: front squat, back squat, sumo squat.

the spine are key. Engage your core and draw your navel inwards.

Inhaling through your nose, lower to a ninety degree angle at your knees and make sure they are both in line with and directly above your toes. A neutral spine must be maintained and if your pelvis begins to tuck under, then ease off as you may need to stretch or strengthen your lower back, hips, hamstrings or calf muscles.

Start position for a squat. Prime movers: quadriceps, gluteus maximus.

Prime movers
quadriceps (thighs), gluteus maximus (bum)

Examples
front squat, back squat, sumo squat

Learn to take responsibility for yourself and your health...

Yasmin Le Bon

Lunge

Stand with your feet hip-width apart, before taking a large step forward. Evenly distribute your weight between both feet and elevate the heel of the trailing foot.

Inhale through your nose and bend your knees. At your lowest point, the front knee should be in line with and directly above your toes. Your trailing knee should drop directly beneath your hip and brush the ground.

Finish position for a lunge. Examples include: front leg elevated lunge, back leg elevated lunge, walking lunge.

Start position for a lunge. Prime movers: hamstrings, quadriceps, gluteus maximus.

Prime movers
quadriceps (thighs), gluteus maximus (bum), hamstrings

Examples
static lunge, walking lunge, backward lunge

Start position for a lift. Prime movers: hamstrings, gluteus maximus.

Finish position for a lift. Examples include: dead lift, Romanian dead lift, clean and press.

Lift

Begin with your feet hip-width apart and toes pointing forwards. Distribute the majority of your weight (70 per cent) into your heels, whilst maintaining a 45-degree angle between your legs and body. As always, you should have a neutral spine and an engaged core. Take a deep breath in through your nose.

On the exhale, push from your heels and lead with your shoulders until you are fully upright. However, be careful not to hyper-extend and maintain soft knees at your finish point.

Prime movers
gluteus maximus (bum), hamstrings

Examples
dead lift, Romanian dead lift, clean and press

Start position for a push. Prime movers: pectoralis major, deltoids, triceps.

Finish position for a push. Examples include: press-up, tricep dip, shoulder press.

Push

Although there are many variations of a push, they are all performed by extending the arms. The angle at which your elbows sit in relation to your body define which prime movers are in control. However, regardless of whether you are pushing up, out or down, it is crucial to keep your core engaged and spine neutral. Also, the muscles that stabilize and support your shoulder blades, known as your scapula, must be active.

Breathe out as you push until your arms reach full extension. Be careful not to hyper-extend or lock your arms aggressively and ensure that your chest is out and your scapula remains depressed to prevent your shoulders rolling forward.

Prime movers
pectoralis major (chest), deltoids (shoulders), triceps

Examples
press-up, tricep dip, shoulder press

Start position for a pull. Prime movers: latissimus dorsi, rhomboids, biceps.

Finish position for a pull. Examples include: overhand chin-up, lateral pull-down, bent-over row.

Pull

Due to the large angle of rotation at the shoulder, there are many variations of pull exercises, but all begin with the arms fully extended. Draw them inwards whilst focusing on a posture that supports your back and complements the motion. A switched-on core and engaged scapula are essential.

Breathe out as you draw your hands towards your body, ensuring the scapula remains depressed, the chest is out and the back isn't arched. The closer the hands get to your body, the more the muscle will be worked.

Technique is especially important when training back muscles.

Prime movers
latissimus dorsi (outer back), rhomboids (centre back), biceps

Examples
chin up, lat pull down, bicep curl

Start position for a rotation. Prime movers: obliques, transverse abdominus.

Finish position for a rotation. Examples include: Russian twists, wood chop, lunge with rotation.

Rotation

Breathe in and ensure you have a neutral, well-supported spine, as well as an engaged core.

Rotate the upper torso on the exhale, but note that the hips must remain static as this reflects an activation of the core muscles.

Once you get to grips with these basic movements, you can move onto larger compound exercises. These are a combination of two or more movements in one fluid motion. For example, a 'full Olympic clean and press' involves a lifting and pulling action to hoist the weight to shoulder level, before squatting and pressing to raise it over your head. Also, smaller movements that isolate muscles are as important and are useful for aesthetics and postural corrections. Bicep curls and side bends are just two examples.

In summary, these movements are so important for balancing the system that neglecting one area will lead to a reduction in progress and increased chance of injury.

Prime movers
obliques, transverse abdominus

Examples
Russian twists, wood chop, lunge with rotation

Remember to work on your posture before you attempt a marathon.

AEROBIC EXERCISE

Examples: jogging, cycling, football, rowing, tennis, skipping.

By engaging in sustained and challenging training, you can significantly improve the efficiency of the body's cardiovascular system. As well as burning fat stores, aerobic exercise is essential for improving and strengthening the heart, lowering blood pressure and increasing the number of red blood cells in the system. This means that each time you exercise, you'll be able to train for longer periods and at a higher intensity.

Initially, aerobic exercise utilizes a chemical reaction known as respiration to convert oxygen and nutritional carbohydrates into energy, carbon dioxide and water. The equation below best illustrates this process.

$$\text{Glucose} + \text{Oxygen} = \text{Carbon Dioxide} + \text{Water} + \text{Energy}$$

After a certain amount of time, the way the body respires changes slightly. Eventually, the available carbohydrates are depleted and so the body begins to metabolize its own fat reserves. This change from dietary to stored sugars is sometimes referred to as 'hitting the

Top exercise tips!

- Dehydration will lead to a 20 per cent drop in performance, so stay hydrated to ensure maximum efficiency.

- A good workout begins with a good night's rest and if you feel too tired to train, then listen to your body.

- However you choose to exercise, ensure your technique is flawless to boost your performance and avoid unnecessary injury.

- Stretching not only improves flexibility but also strengthens and tones the muscles as well.

- Vary your routine to always keep the body guessing. Experiment with new activities, exercises and intensities.

- One-legged exercises can help with core strength and restore equilibrium throughout the muscles, but be extra careful to ensure a good technique.

- If you work one muscle, it is crucial to exercise its opposing counterpart. This is key to a balanced body.

wall'. Therefore, in order to get the most benefit from aerobic exercise, you really should train for a minimum of forty-five minutes, allowing enough time for the body to make the shift from dietary carbohydrates to stored fat.

One of the fastest ways to do this is to engage in high-intensity interval training. This involves four minutes of high intensity exercise where your heart rate is at 80 per cent of its maximum, followed by a one-minute recovery period. Your maximum heart rate can be calculated using something called the 'in-bar' formula.

Maximum Heart Rate $= 205.8 - 0.685 \times$ Age

From this equation, you can calculate 80 per cent of your maximum heart rate by dividing by 100 and then multiplying the answer by 80. It is the same for men and women. Don't worry if this seems complicated; the table below contains a list maximum heart rates and 80 per cent of that figure for a range of ages.

Age	Maximum heart rate (bpm)	80 per cent of maximum heart rate (bpm)
18	193	154
19	193	154
20	192	153
21	191	152
22	190	152
23	190	152
24	189	151
25	188	150
26	187	150
27	187	150
28	186	149
29	185	148
30	185	148

It is not recommended that you exercise when you are hungry and always complement your exercise with a well-balanced diet. Whilst training on an empty stomach might seem like a short-cut to burning fat sooner, the body's chemistry will be nowhere near as effective. It would be the equivalent of trying to run a mile without breathing; if all the elements of the equation aren't present, the system simply shuts down.

Be aware that lengthy bouts of aerobic activities such as road-running can have negative repercussions for the joints, so ensure you have the correct footwear and vary your exercise to include activities like cycling and swimming. These are great way to burn fat without placing your muscles and joints under undue stress.

REST AND RECOVERY

Rest days and restful nights ensure the body has enough time to recover and are essential for any well-balanced exercise routine. Overtraining is unhealthy and can even be dangerous, making downtime just as important as the exercise itself. As well as not repaying the oxygen debt, the side effects of pushing your body too hard include the release of various hormones that upset the system's delicate balance and a greater chance of illness and injury. Similarly, plenty of sleep is recommended. Protein synthesis occurs most efficiently at night and without this, the body begins to shut down, reducing visible results.

In summary, working as a model comes with the pressure of having a good figure, but, with the right attitude, your daily workout will become a privilege that others simply don't have the time for. The key to being in good shape is to apply a healthy balance to the way you exercise. Firstly, everyone needs a balanced diet that allows them to train with energy and vigour. Next, regardless of your goals, you need to balance your skeleton with postural exercises, strengthen your core muscles and improve flexibility. Postural exercises, core work and stretching can all be performed at home, in a hotel room or wherever modelling happens to take you.

Finally, incorporate a range of movements to engage all of the body's muscles and that includes your heart. Like everything in life, balance is the key to success and devising a well-balanced programme will ensure you get the most out of your time and effort.

Tailor your rest days depending on the type and intensity of your exercise routine, but it is recommended you take at least one or two rest days a week.

SKINCARE

The way you treat your skin can make a big difference to your look, confidence and longevity as a model because good skin reflects physical and psychological well-being. Potential clients will either consciously, or unknowingly, gauge a model's diet, stress levels, sleep patterns and general lifestyle via their complexion. Furthermore, this instantaneous decision can last, making it important to present yourself as a healthy and well-balanced individual. Also, attending castings with bad skin, even if it is well concealed, may affect personal confidence, making a skincare regime all the more important. Although make-up, spot treatments and cosmetic procedures can remedy facial acne, bags or dark circles under the eyes and signs of premature ageing, it is far better to

focus on prevention and daily maintenance. Just like exercise routines and meal plans, skin care regimes are unique to the individual and depending on your age, skin type, allergies, diet and lifestyle, your daily routines may vary. There are, however, some factors that can significantly improve your skin tone on both your face and body.

The first of these is a person's nutrition, because almost 30 per cent of internal toxins are excreted through our pores. Therefore, eating too much sugary food is likely to cause increased facial acne. Specifically, pimples forming between the eyebrows are probably the result of a bad daily diet and can be easily prevented by cutting out refined carbohydrates and hydrogenated fats. A healthy diet is also beneficial for improving the elasticity of the skin.

I love fashion, but I'm not obsessed with it.
Christy Turlington

Eating plenty of fruit and vegetables helps the skin to get the vitamins it needs for repair. In addition, antioxidants found in vegetables protect skin from the damaging effects of sunlight as well as reduce inflammation and neutralize cell-damaging agents. Also, drinking enough fluids cleans the pores from the inside, rehydrates the skin and increases its suppleness.

There are some instances where even healthy foods can cause problems. For example, acne across the forehead may be as a result of the system struggling to digest a certain food type. If you find that you break out in this area whenever you eat a specific meal, then try avoiding it and measure your skin's response.

As well as diet and digestive problems, hormone imbalances can lead to spots, particularly around the mouth, on the nose and the chin, and on the chest and back. This is especially apparent in your teens, although facial acne affects many people for years after they reach puberty. The contraceptive pill, pregnancy and menstrual cycle can also affect a woman's skin. Persistent problems in these areas are best discussed with a doctor and certain medications can help. You should also consult your doctor if you are having problems with recurrent acne on your cheeks. This may indicate underlying stomach problems or may be an early sign of stress.

On top of internal factors, the quality of your skin also depends on how effectively you remove dirt, make-up and dead skin cells, restore the skin's natural pH balance and reintroduce moisture. This is especially important if you live in a big, polluted city where blocked pores require constant attention.

The four steps to great skin are to cleanse, exfoliate tone and moisturize. On top of these, there are a few things to avoid that will prevent premature ageing and acne.

FACIAL SKINCARE ROUTINE
Cleanse
Cleansing twice a day should be enough, but it is important to buy a cleanser that suits your skin type. You

Every now and then, a face mask can bring an extra radiance to your skin.

should always wash your face with warm water, because if the temperature is too hot or too cold, capillaries just under the skin can break, causing redness or swelling. Use either a mild cleanser or antibacterial wash that reacts favourably with your skin and always be careful not to scrub too hard. Instead, gently employ circular motions allowing the active ingredients in the soap to remove excess oil and dirt, before gently towelling your face dry. Alternatively, cream cleansers are just as effective at dirt removal and are perhaps better suited to dryer skin types.

Most shop assistants should be able to help you with regard to how strong a cleanser you will need, but the best people to ask are the make-up artists you meet on jobs. They will have seen and worked with a spectrum of skin types and are full of handy tips and advice. Also, the better quality your skin is, the easier their task is, so never be afraid or embarrassed to ask about their products.

Exfoliate

Exfoliating the skin not only removes dirt and unblocks pores, but is a great way to discard dead skin cells and brighten your complexion. Whilst some recommend exfoliating on a weekly basis, others suggest it should be part of your daily skincare regime. The right answer probably lies somewhere in the middle, so exfoliate every couple of days or when you feel like your skin needs a boost.

Tone

Water disrupts the skin's natural pH balance and although the skin naturally restores this level unaided, it can take up to fourteen hours. Beauty therapists therefore recommend a good toner as an immediate remedy after cleansing. However, it is important to avoid using a toner that contains alcohol as this strips the skin of its natural oils, known as sebum, and leads to dry skin. In response, pores secrete excess sebum to compensate, which can cause breakouts and oily patches.

Top Skincare Tips!

- Cleanse, tone and moisturize. Always in that order and at least twice a day.

- Always remember to exfoliate moist skin as this avoids unnecessary damage.

- Never neglect your neck. Exfoliating and moisturizing this area is just as important as your face.

- If you must squeeze a spot, then prepare the area with hot water to open the pores and use tissue paper or a cotton bud to soften the trauma. Immediately after, use cold water to close the pores and prevent infection.

- Good skin starts from within, so make sure you eat well and drink plenty of water.

Moisturize

Once the dirt is removed from your skin, it is essential to focus on reintroducing moisture as well as minimizing the effects of sun damage. In fact, most beauty therapists agree that application of sunscreen or a moisturizer with a minimum SPF of 15 is the most important part of your daily skincare regimen. Although spots come and go, wrinkles are a lot harder to shift and, therefore, a moisturizing sunscreen should be applied even during winter or on cloudy days. A word of caution: be careful not to use sunscreen or a moisturizer with an SPF at night, as the ingredients are not designed to be used constantly. Instead, before bed apply a cream that seals in moisture. Then when you wake, splash your face with tepid water as a way of removing the excess oils from your nightly moisturizing. Also, have a large glass of water to hydrate the skin from within.

Eye creams are sometimes recommended to add additional moisture to an area that has less fatty tissue and is, therefore, more susceptible to wrinkles. However, some skin experts feel that a good moisturizer should be enough and this is a matter of personal preference.

PREVENT PREMATURE AGEING AND ACNE WITH GENERAL MAINTENANCE

Neglecting your skin earlier in life can have a massive impact later on, so as well as a daily routine, a healthy diet and plenty of water, there are also plenty of things to avoid.

Avoid Ultraviolet (UV) Damage

By avoiding tanning, unnecessary exposure to the sun and never using sunbeds, you can prevent the harmful effects of ultraviolet light. With so many good-quality tinted moisturizers and natural spray tans on the market,

I know a model who ...

turned up to a job, having been up all night. The make-up artist had to spend ages making her look half-decent. The client didn't notice, but the stylist and grooming team never recommend her.

Stay out of the sun and model for years to come.

there is no need to risk your skin's health by forcefully blasting it with radiation. Equally, and especially when shooting in hot climates, be conscious of overheating and sweating under make-up, because this leads to blocked pores, heat rashes and breakouts. Instead, opt for the shade and have smooth, wrinkle-free skin for longer.

Smoking

Smoking, drinking and drug use should be avoided, because poisons in your body will almost immediately be reflected in the quality of your skin. Premature wrinkles and bags or dark circles under the eyes will constantly blight a person who engages in these types of destructive behaviour. Also, unhealthy activities cause undue stress and disrupt sleep patterns, further adding to the problem. In contrast, a consistent exercise plan helps to keep your complexion clear and your skin looking fresh and energized.

Make-up Removal

Try to avoid using make-up unless it is necessary. For example, a trip to the supermarket or gym doesn't require the same amount of make-up as a fashion show. When you have been using cosmetics, another point to remember is the importance of giving your skin a rest whenever you can. Therefore, always, without fail, remove your make-up before you go to bed.

Overall, these daily or twice-daily routines can make skincare feel like a lot of effort, but once a balance is found, skincare is actually very easy, inexpensive and considerably less effort than having to worry about spots, dry skin or the signs of premature ageing. A strict regime is even more important if you hope to have longevity as a model, because staying naturally youthful-looking will ensure work for years to come. The key is to engage good practices like cleansing, exfoliating, moisturizing and eating sensibly from a young age. Remember that the skin is the body's largest organ and poor overall health will always counteract the effects of even the most diligent skincare routines. Keeping good habits in addition to good skincare will help the skin age gracefully and beautifully, but don't panic about your skin quality as stress only serves to exacerbate the situation. Digital retouching can take care of even the most unsightly of blemishes, so stay confident.

The face you have at age twenty-five is the face God gave you, but the face you have after fifty is the face you earned.

Cindy Crawford

BODY MAINTENANCE

Although a model's face is always on display, you may also be required to show your hands, feet and body at a moment's notice. Therefore, looking after yourself completely means paying attention to everything from the soles of your feet to your bikini line. Just like the skin on your face, you should regularly cleanse, exfoliate and moisturize the skin on your body. In addition, both girls and boys should focus on hair removal and finger and toenail maintenance.

WASH

Using your shower time carefully can ensure bright, healthy-looking skin. Firstly, if possible, shower before you go to bed as this removes the day's dirt and helps your pores to remain unblocked all night long. In the shower use a soap or body wash that reacts kindly with your skin and use a good-quality sponge or loofah rather than just cleaning by hand. As well as being more effective at removing dirt, sponges and loofahs simultaneously exfoliate the skin, removing dead cells that could potentially block the pores. A great way to open the pores is to use a sauna or steam bath. Five or ten minutes in a sauna, followed by a cold shower and thorough clean can really improve your skin's appearance as you sweat out both internal and external pollutants. If you do use a sauna, be careful to drink plenty of water before, during and after to ensure you stay hydrated.

EXFOLIATE

It is important to use an exfoliating scrub two or three times a week. As well as removing the layer of dead skin, it stimulates the regeneration of new skin by encouraging blood flow to the surface. Exfoliating also prepares the skin below for moisturizing, shaving or the use of a self-tan cream. After showering, take a spoon of body scrub and even it out by rubbing between the palms of your hands. Then, gently massage the skin in circular motions before rinsing off with warm water.

Exfoliating body scrubs can be expensive and claim to possess all manner of beneficial properties, but most are a combination of perfume, oils and sea salt. Here is a

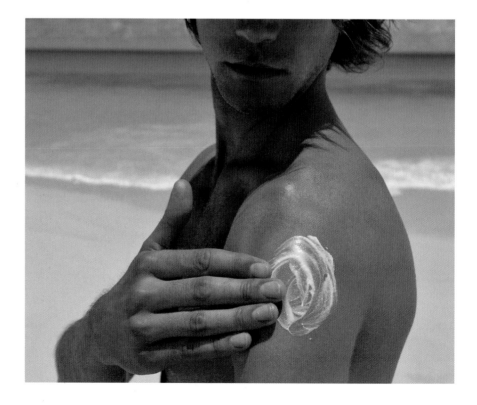

Protect your skin, because it is your body's largest organ.

Prevent unsightly callouses on the palms of your hands by wearing gym gloves during your daily workout.

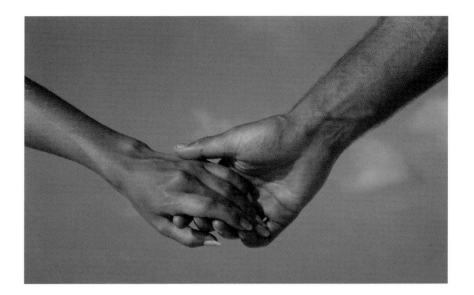

Remove dead skin from your feet with a pumice stone. You never know when they'll be in shot.

Home-made body scrub

Ingredients

½ cup of sea salt from a grocery store
½ cup of coconut oil
½ cup of coarse brown sugar
3 teaspoons of organic dark cocoa powder
½ teaspoon of vanilla extract
½ teaspoon of coconut extract

Preparation

1. Mix the salt, oils and sugar in a glass jar until the consistency is right. It should be thick, but not dry.

2. Slowly mix in the cocoa powder.

3. Seal the jar and store in the fridge.

I know a model who …

got so sunburned on a trip to the Caribbean that she had to be sent home.

sunbathing or sunbeds. If you are in the sun, then you must take care not to get burnt. Use a high SPF lotion and seek shade whenever possible. This is especially important on shoots because sunburnt skin looks too red in photographs. Furthermore, if a model cannot shoot because of the crippling effects of sunburn, the client will not be pleased. Repeatedly burning your skin is dangerous and significantly increases the chance of developing melanoma.

NAIL CARE

It's very common for models to have to show their hands at castings. Nails need not be perfectly manicured at all times, but they should be clean and trimmed, and this goes for your toenails too. The key here is to get into a routine where you trim and file your nails and tidy your cuticles.

By performing these tasks at least once a week, you

recipe for a home-made body scrub that is just as effective as any high street equivalent, but costs a fraction of the price.

MOISTURIZE AND PROTECT

A good body moisturizer is essential for supple, youthful-looking skin. Use a tinted moisturizer as an alternative to

You can never predict how close it will get, so ensure you're ready for anything.

A good razor, shaving cream and brush are important, and keeping the face well hydrated is essential.

can feel confident when shaking potential clients' hands or if asked to go barefoot at a casting. Girls are advised to stick to neutral nail colours and natural nails are preferable to artificial ones. Boys should think about removing or reducing hair on fingers and toes.

HAIR REMOVAL

When it comes to body hair, as a rule less is more. For girls, legs, armpits and bikini lines should always be hair-free, and for boys, unless it is intrinsic to your look, a hairless torso is preferred. Shaving, waxing and hair removal creams are all viable solutions and how you remove hair is a personal choice, just as long as you remove it. After all, you can be asked remove your clothes at castings and on jobs with no notice, so it is important to always be prepared.

SHAVING

Most male models prefer to manage their stubble using a beard trimmer or clippers, but a correctly executed clean shave gives your pores a chance to breathe. Furthermore, a close shave can transform your image in just a few minutes, allowing you to present clients with an alternative look that may be exactly what they want. However, shaving incorrectly can cause bleeding, skin irritation and breakouts, making the perfect shave something all male models should strive for.

The perfect shave requires the right tools and the most vital piece of equipment, surprisingly, is not the razor. Whilst the type of blade is important, and you may be inclined to use a double-edge safety razor instead of a multi-blade cartridge razor, it is a high-calibre shaving brush that is really essential. Add a shaving brush to your kit and you'll immediately notice the difference. In addition, you will need good-quality shaving cream, facial exfoliating scrub and a cleansing lotion containing witch hazel. The final ingredient needed is plenty of water, because the more hydrated your face is before, during and after your shave, the closer and more comfortable it will be.

Preparation

Before you apply the cream or even think about getting the razor near your face, you need to prepare the skin and soften the hair. The best way to do this is with a hot shower to open the skin pores and this is the reason that professional barbers use hot towels. Whilst in the shower, use the facial exfoliating scrub to remove the layer of dead skin and further soften the hairs. Meanwhile, allow your shaving brush to soak in a sink full of hot water. Once out of the shower, remove the brush and allow the excess water to drain off so that it is wet, but manageable. Similarly, don't towel off your face, but if you need to dab your forehead or dry your hair to prevent water dripping down your face then feel free to do so.

Shaving

Take the brush and use it to apply the shaving cream with circular motions until a healthy lather has built up. Take your time and ensure the area around the jaw and neck are completely covered. Then slowly use the razor to shave the hair and remember to always shave in the direction the stubble is growing. Just like the hairs on your head, facial whiskers grow in all manner of directions and shaving with the grain reduces irritation and the chances of ingrowing hair. This process can take several minutes and should not be rushed. Another point to note is that if you decide on a double-edge safety razor as opposed to a multi-blade cartridge razor, then under no circumstances should you apply pressure on

I know a model who …

refused to shave his beard because he needed it for his next job. He got sent home and replaced.

your face. The benefit of these razors is the blade's sharpness and the lighter your touch, the closer the shave. Applying pressure will only serve to cut the skin, so be warned.

Post-shave

Once you are satisfied with the closeness of your shave, immediately rinse your face with cold water to close the pores and don't forget to rinse off your shaving brush and dispose of the razor blade. Dab your face dry before using a cotton pad soaked in a cleansing lotion containing witch hazel to ensure minimal inflammation and to stop any nicks becoming infected. Finally, use your daily moisturizer to ensure your face remains hydrated.

Overall, a double-edge safety razor instead of a multi-blade cartridge or disposable razor will give you the closest shave, but it you prefer not to switch, then you should at least use a shaving brush. Finally, many of the same principles apply to girls when shaving their legs, armpits and bikini lines. Remember to open and clean the pores, shave with the grain and always keep the skin well hydrated.

TATTOOS

It's generally not advisable to get tattoos if you have chosen a career in modelling. The majority of the time a visible tattoo will only hinder your chances of getting a job. Tattoo-concealing make-up, flesh-coloured material and post-production retouching are all options, but are also time-consuming and expensive processes, resulting in many clients simply casting a model without a tattoo. This is particularly significant for commercial models, because tattoos not only send out a message, they also distract from the product or image the client is hoping to portray. Alternatively, some high fashion editorials and campaigns might desire a tattoo and actively seek out models with body art. However, body paints, transfers and fake tattoos are all readily available, making it easier to add them rather than hide them. Nonetheless, a tattoo can be a part of a model's look and many in the industry are adamant that it doesn't affect their ability to book work. One market where it will definitely affect you is Tokyo. Here, tattoos are linked with the Japanese Mafia, so models are often asked to hide them on jobs and castings. In the gym people are asked to cover them up.

If you do decide to commission a tattoo, it's advisable to consider its design, size and placement carefully, because tattoos are a lot like accessories and what is fashionable now might look dated next year. Settle on a style that is either personal or makes a statement about who you are. A compromise might be to have a small tattoo placed where it can be easily concealed, for example at the nape of the neck. Finally, if you have a tattoo prior to entering into the modelling world and you feel it might hinder you, then arrive at castings and jobs with it already concealed.

There are also laser removal treatments available. Speak to your agent and see what they recommend.

Tattoos can form part of a model's look and even help define their identity.

PIERCINGS

Face

Facial piercings are usually not a problem as long as they can be removed easily. Once out, most piercings leave a tiny hole that can either be passed off as a freckle or retouched if the camera is particularly close. In fact, most female models have their ears pierced because earrings are often considered accessories to many outfits. Therefore, a model without pierced ears might actually lose out on jewellery campaigns or catalogues. However, multiple ear piercings can misshape the helix or the outer ear and beauty models should steer clear of lip, nose and eyebrow piercings. Use your judgement and remove less conventional piercings when attending more commercial castings.

Body

Body piercings are often concealed at castings and therefore are only relevant for lingerie and swimwear work or when the clothing is extremely tight-fitting. On these occasions a client might request that a nipple or navel piercing be removed and if this is not possible, the client should be made aware in advance.

Extreme piercings are inappropriate for most commercial clients, although there are model agencies that specialize in extreme, abstract and character modelling.

HAIR CARE

Typically, a model's hair should be thick, glossy and bursting with vitality. However, as a model, your hair is regularly exposed to a host of damaging treatments in addition to the daily wear and tear of washing, blow-drying and sun damage. Heated appliances and products cause dehydration and techniques like back-combing

I know a model who ...

didn't have a tidy bikini line on a lingerie shoot. The client had to tell her to go to the bathroom and shave. At first, she refused and made a big deal out of it. Eventually, she gave in, but the atmosphere in the studio was horrid for the rest of the day.

A model's hair goes through all sorts of treatment, so be sure to give it a rest when you can.

can lead to hair being brittle or weak. Furthermore, frequent colour changes strip the hair of natural oils, which can often result in thinning, leading to the need for extensions. Worse still, the application and removal of extensions can lead to yet more damage. Therefore, for all of these reasons, it is in your best interest to care for and protect your hair as best you can.

Haircare begins with a balanced, nutritious diet and then extends to good general maintenance. Selenium, found in seafood, Brazil nuts and quinoa, and vitamin B2, found in mushrooms, broccoli and eggs, are just two examples of dietary nutrients that will have a positive effect on your hair. From there, a good-quality shampoo and conditioner are a must, and although you should wash and condition your hair frequently, this should not be an everyday occurrence. Washing your hair too often strips the natural oils from the hair.

Prior to wetting, gently comb your hair through, removing any knots or tangles. This action also spreads the hair's natural oils, making it appear shinier and healthier. In contrast, combing your hair when wet is not advised because, in this state, it is most vulnerable to damage. Then, wash your hair by working the lather from roots to ends and always massage your scalp well with your fingertips, before rinsing with cool water to help seal the cuticle and lock in more shine.

Regular conditioning treatments will retain moisture and help restore hair to its best condition, and so frequent use is advisable for all hair types. However, don't condition your roots. The roots are close to the oil glands that provide plenty of lubrication; they also don't get damaged like the rest of the tresses. If you are prone to greasy hair, avoiding conditioner on the roots will also help to lessen the appearance of oily hair. Apply conditioner at the nape of your neck and work up and through hair, concentrating on the ends.

Whenever possible, use a heat protection spray and minimize the use of heated appliances in your personal life. Just like your skin, it's good to give your hair a break because the more successful you are, the more abuse your hair will encounter on jobs. By not allowing it time to recover, its condition can rapidly deteriorate.

A common problem is split ends, which hamper the growth of hair and also gives the tips of each strand a white, coarse appearance. To reduce the appearance of split ends, have your hair cut regularly. This doesn't have to be an extreme shortening or a complete change of style and a light trim should suffice. Many agencies have relationships with hair salons that provide their services at reduced rates or even for free. Alternatively, politely ask the hairstylist on photo shoots or at fashion shows to take a few extra minutes to deal with any split ends.

Dyed hair, highlights or lowlights are another area to consider. If you do change your hair colour, it is your

I know a model who …

ate so little, her hair started to fall out.

personal responsibility to keep the colour looking fresh and always ensure that it matches the photographs in your portfolio. Also, you may have request castings or options in the near future and if you change your look, you may jeopardize your chances of securing the work, making it good practice to check with your agent before dyeing your hair. Try to avoid bleaching as this makes the hair shaft brittle and porous. Bleached hair can be dry and more likely to break. Naturally fair hair is best lightened with a dye or a high lift tint instead of bleach to reduce the chances of damage and dehydration.

Overall, the kind of hair most prone to damage is long, fine, colour-treated hair. Most hair can cope with day-to-day life, but avoid blow-drying too often and frequent use of straightening irons or tongs, and refrain from back-combing. When shooting, stylists may use any of these methods and even the most robust hair can show signs of neglect. Also, avoid chlorine, wear a hat in the sun and hold back on bleaching. Treat it with care and you'll be rewarded with shiny, healthy hair.

EXTENSIONS

Often in photo shoots the key to fabulous hair is the clever use of hair extensions which are carefully blended to match the model's own hair. Hair extensions offer instant volume, thicken out empty ends and can provide emergency relief from a disastrous haircut. Many stylists carry a variety of colours and types to most jobs, but because every person's hair is unique, it makes sense to provide your own extensions, aiding the hairstylist and, more importantly, ensuring the extensions are undetectable.

When searching for the best extensions to suit your hair, there are two main methods to consider: clip-in extensions and semi-permanent extensions. In addition, you may consider a weave or a wig, and depending on your hair type, budget and lifestyle, any of these methods might be more appropriate for you.

Semi-permanent Extensions

Semi-permanent extensions are bonded to the natural hair strands using a variety of professional techniques, and this is both a costly and lengthy process. Once in position, the extensions usually last three to four months, and during that time the new strands can be washed and

dried along with your natural hair. They also appear natural because they are extensions of a small section of hair rather than a block addition, but on the downside most stylists find working with semi-permanent extensions difficult because the delicate nature of the bond prevents pulling too hard during blow-drying. Another disadvantage is the possibility of traction alopecia caused primarily by the pulling force being applied to the hair. Overall, semi-permanent extensions are better for people with thicker hair, who are hoping to add length and who have the patience and budget to renew the extensions four times a year.

Clip-in Extensions

Clip-in extensions are ideally suited to people with thin hair hoping to add volume and represent a more cost-effective solution. They can be added in minutes, removed even faster and, after use, washed and hung out to dry. Clip-in extensions also avoid the damage caused by bonding glue sometimes used when attaching semi-permanent extensions, although you are not likely to enjoy the round-the-clock benefits or natural movement of bonded extensions. For example, if shooting on location or with a wind machine, gusts can reveal the separate block of hair and sometimes the top of the weft. In summary, clip-in extensions offer an instant solution and, in an industry where versatility is a must, this is a great way to change your look at little extra cost.

Weave

Small sections of your own hair are braided close to the scalp in approximately three rows around the head for a full lot of hair extensions. These braids form an attachment area to which a curtain of false hair is then sewn. This method is better suited to thicker, coarser hair. A weave is somewhat restrictive as tying the hair back can be difficult and it doesn't tend to look as natural as other methods.

Wig

A wig is very restrictive, but if it is of good quality and it is well styled, can be good for castings and some jobs.

Whichever method you decide on, take your time to find extensions of identical colour, length and texture to your own hair and if you can afford it, buy real, virgin

smaller bust. The ideal is considered to be 34B and if additional cup sizes are needed during a shoot or show, then chicken fillets, padded bras and post-production retouching make a minimal chest unproblematic for most girls. In addition, a particularly voluptuous model might not be booked for a job because high fashion models working on editorial shoots and shows are often required to wear sheer fabrics, backless dresses and go without the support of a bra. Also, fittings and show-room models might be overlooked if the clothes don't sit well around the chest.

In contrast, smaller-chested models might lose work because of their cup size and although they can have their bust temporarily or digitally enhanced, curves are viewed as a desirable quality for many catalogue, lifestyle and television clients. A typically feminine look is also required for lingerie and swimwear work and most underwear clients expect their girls to fill at least a B-cup. Glamour girls are also generally expected to have a fuller bust and many girls in this area, who have the support of their friends and family, feel implants to be a good investment.

With such contrasting views on cup size, it might seem difficult to figure out where you fit in and whether the girls with larger or smaller busts are likely to be more successful. The answer probably lies somewhere in between and as long as your breasts look natural and in proportion, the quality and frequency of your work should not suffer. A model who regularly books jobs, but consistently loses out on lingerie jobs or swimwear work solely because of her cup size, might feel she is a viable candidate for surgery. It is simply a case of assessing how much more work she believes she is likely to get and to what extent her personal life will be affected. On the other hand, if a girl decides to have an operation for personal reasons, the chances of her implants negatively affecting her career are small as long the results are natural and stay in proportion with the rest of her body shape. However, an unsuccessful model who thinks implants will dramatically boost her career is mistaken and quick fixes are rarely the answer. Either way, this decision requires time and thought and should be made by no one else but you.

In summary, cosmetic surgery of any type is a big step and you should therefore never feel pressured into a decision about changing your physical appearance. With make-up, clever lighting and digital post-production, minor imperfections are best ignored. If a physical trait is affecting your personal confidence so detrimentally that, even after discussion with friends, family and bookers, it just cannot be ignored any longer, then maybe a cosmetic procedure could help. After all, the reflection you see in the mirror is something that should not cause undue stress. However, there are risks to every procedure and, as a result, a lot of thought and consideration should go into whether going under the knife is the best option. There are also occasions where surgery is really not advised and if a model is considering liposuction, a breast enlargement or muscle implants because they believe their career will change considerably as a result, then, on the whole, they are mistaken. Seek the opinion of medical professionals on the full financial, physical and emotional costs.

MAKE-UP

A model should be able to apply a good basic make-up and it is skill that requires subtlety. Your look for cast-

Striking make-up can transform a photograph.

For castings and everyday life, less is more. You'll look younger, fresher and appear effortless.

ings should always be simple, clean and natural unless the brief requires you to add a touch more colour. The key is to enhance your natural features, whilst disguising any imperfections, and all with the appearance of effortlessness.

Start by experimenting at home in varying light conditions before venturing to castings and, if you can, apply your make-up in natural light to give you a true idea of how it looks. Often, make-up appears different under studio lights and on camera, so the less you apply, the less risk there is. When out and about, carry a small basic make-up kit with you for minimal changes, to freshen up between castings and reduce the shine caused by travelling across a large city.

THE BASICS

Start with a clean, dry face and apply moisturizer with a minimum 15 SPF to hydrate and protect your skin. You

may choose to use an illuminating and highlighting cream that can be mixed with your moisturizer, but either way, allow it to soak in for a few minutes. A liquid foundation should always be applied with a make-up sponge to prevent any dirt from your fingers clogging your pores. Softly dab the sponge as you work across your face rather than smearing the foundation as this gives a more even finish. Remember not to stop at your jaw line but to continue onto your neck and chest for a seamless blend with your natural skin tone.

If you have blemishes that require the use of a concealer, then again it is crucial to apply the make-up with a brush and not with your fingers. Use a high pigment concealer and work it in until it has blended with your skin. Use a light-reflecting, thinner concealer under your eyes, either side of your nose and mouth. Lightly dab with a sponge to bind with the skin and foundation.

Practice makes perfect, so don't give up.

Bright/dark lips are best complemented with clean and natural eyes.

Once you have an even skin tone, enhancing your bone structure with a little bronzer lightly brushed along your hairline, down either side of your face and under your chin can really help. Often, it is enough to simply stroke once under each cheekbone. Additional contouring can be achieved with a lighter blush directly on the cheekbones and a dab on the nose and chin.

Before you move onto defining your eyes, apply a loose powder just under each one so that any falling shadow can be easily cleaned off. For a natural eye, use a nude, beige or natural eyeshadow. Take your brush and begin on your lids just above the lash line. After your

I love the confidence that make-up gives me.
Tyra Banks

initial application, no additional eyeshadow is needed. Instead, work the brush up towards your brow, blending it as you go. For slightly more definition, use a slightly darker eyeshadow but be careful not to add too much. Also, a dark eye pencil can add vigour to the eyes and boost the impact of your lashes. Make sure the pencil is sharp and carefully apply it where your lashes meet the eyelid; you may find that a series of dots are easier to manage than a continuous line.

Managing your brows is equally important and when plucking, remember never to pluck from the top of the brow, only from underneath. To add depth to your brows, use an eyebrow pencil with short, feathery strokes to create the desired shape; sparse areas can be strengthened by brushing upwards with a hint of eyeshadow, a clear mascara or brow-setter.

Once you are happy with your eye definition, foundation and contour, use a powder to eliminate any shine, but be careful not to use too much as this will age skin. A great way to prevent over-application is to place a fine tissue over the area as you brush on the powder. This acts as a filter, prevents powder sitting in the contours of the skin and leaves you with a fine and even finish.

Lastly, a neutral lip colour is generally the most appropriate for castings, making a moisturizing lip balm enough. Apply generously before blotting any excess on a sheet of tissue paper.

To get smoky eyes, use dark pencil eyeliner to bring out your eyes. Choose eyeshadows in rich browns and

Top Make-up Tips!

- Dramatic eyes or dramatic lips. Never both!
- Avoid heavy concealer under your eyes and restrict the use of powder, as it can make your skin appear dull and lifeless.
- Add a flush of colour to your cheeks and a dab of balm to your lips for an instant freshen-up.
- Add a touch of highlighter to the outside of each cheekbone for a more glamorous look.
- Good-quality foundation is important.
- With cosmetics, you get what you pay for.

deep greys and blend the colour a little higher on the brow bone. Apply black pencil eyeliner to the inside border of the lower eyelid. For a little bit of a 'cat's eyes' look, extend the liner just slightly past the outer corner of your eye, taking it upward. Apply a coat of black mascara to your eyelashes.

If you do want to wear more colour, use a lip liner and gently blend from the outside in. Put a dab of gloss in the middle to give the appearance of fuller lips.

Ultimately, being able to personally apply good make-up makes a world of difference when trying to secure work, and sometimes even on jobs themselves. If in doubt, remember that when it comes to make-up, less is most certainly more.

CLOTHING, ACCESSORIES AND STYLING

Wearing whatever you like is fine for your personal life and you may have cherished items of clothing and accessories that come together to define your easily identifiable look. However, as a model you need to view styling in a slightly different way because, quite often, the clothes you wear will not necessarily represent you as a person. Instead, when attending castings your daily attire should reflect the character you are trying to convey and whilst you should retain a degree of individuality, it is more important to shape your image in the way that is most likely to secure you the job. Therefore, your primary indicator of how to dress should be the brief provided by your agent. Sometimes

Great legs? Then show them off! However, you shouldn't wear hot pants or a miniskirt every time you leave the house.

on the casting notes the client will specify exact items of clothing they would like you to wear, but in the absence of any direct information, gauge what the client or photographer will be looking for. For example, when casting for a catalogue client, you should dress neutrally and err on the side of smart casual, as they will not be expecting the sort of urban look or hyper-trendy styling that belongs on an editorial. Similarly, turning up to a clothing campaign casting with a rival brand's logo splashed across your chest will not score you points with the client.

Secondly, and equally as important as shaping your image towards expectation, is to always dress in a way that makes you feel confident about who you are. This is never more relevant than when trying to incorporate the latest trends into your look. Remember that fashions are always changing and with so much variation, you cannot guarantee that each season's trend will suit you perfectly or highlight your most appealing features. Therefore, stubbornly sticking with the trend until it fades from the high street could mean months of you neither looking nor feeling your best. For example, if trousers or long skirts are the season's look and you have fantastic legs, opting for either could mean hiding one of your best assets for up to half a year.

Muscular boys shouldn't be tempted to wear tight-fitting, low-cut T-shirts everywhere they go as some clients find the look intimidating and bordering on vain. Most of all, poor styling or over-accessorizing just draws attention away from you and can mean the difference between being confirmed for a job or not.

A picture is already emerging of what a model's style should be and words like effortlessness, confidence, versatility, subtlety and timelessness will help you feel great about the image you are displaying, regardless of the clothes you are actually wearing. What's more, finding what works for you will help you avoid costly

Save money by adding personal touches to basic outfits, but be careful not to over-accessorize.

errors when trying to be fashionable on a budget. If you are stuck for inspiration, then turn to fashion magazines and take note of what is being worn by fashionable celebrities. Speak to the stylists on jobs and pay attention to the outfits they dress you in, the colours and textures they use to complement your skintone, body shape and hair colour as well as the way they accessorize you to bring a simple look to life.

Once you have an idea of what your style is, you need to back it up with the right clothing and that will probably mean a trip to the high street. Although you must be careful about wasting money, it is important that your clothes are always in good condition. Old, tatty, clothing is never a good look and regardless how comfortable a piece is, or what sentimental memories it holds for you,

I know a model who ...

wore Puma trainers on an Adidas job, not knowing about the massive rivalry between the two companies. The client made him take off the shoes, set fire to them and never booked him again!

if it is worn out, then it must be discarded. After all, a model's job is to look great and what you wear and the way you wear it says a lot about your personality. Furthermore, working in the fashion industry comes with the added pressure to dress well every time you leave the house in a professional capacity. Save your oldest and most favourite jumper for a Sunday afternoon trip to the supermarket.

FASHION ON A BUDGET

When shopping for clothes, remember that quality doesn't need to be reflected in the price tag. Many top designers and fashion forward celebrities are collaborating with high street stores to bring credibility to the brand and, therefore, affordable and fashionable clothing at reasonable prices. Whilst designer clothes undoubtedly look cutting edge, a similar look can be achieved for a fraction of the price by shopping on the high street.

Online shopping has taken a leap forward in the last few years and, currently, chic clothing and the latest accessories are available around the clock and mostly with free delivery and returns. Furthermore, there are websites dedicated to recreating current trends and ways to imitate highly priced designer goods on a budget, as well as blogs that offer a constantly updated encyclopedia of advice and teams of people allocated solely to scouting the streets for the must-haves of the season.

Of course, the only disadvantage to shopping online is that you cannot try the items on, and sometimes the way an item appears in the photograph is very different to its appearance, fit and feel in real life. Therefore, if you have the time and patience, find a garment you like on the high street, try it on for size and take note of its unique product code. Then in the comfort of your own home you can search cyberspace for the garment's counterpart, potentially saving a great deal of money. Even if you save only 10 per cent on each piece of clothing you buy, this can represent a significant annual saving.

> *The expression a woman wears on her face is more important than the clothes she wears on her back.*
>
> Dale Carnegie

Vintage clothing will always be sought after, as it boasts exclusivity and originality, but again, it is not a privilege you need to pay too much for. Searching second-hand shops and consignment stores can result in a great bargain as well as a good story, as long as you have the patience to sort the deals from the duds. Alternatively, there are times when spending a bit extra on a key piece can be worth the investment. These items should represent your core style and be able to stay in your wardrobe from year to year. Good-quality garments, with fine workmanship, fabrics and perhaps intricate detailing, are worth the extra money, provided they are timeless and represent you and your style. Similarly, footwear is an area where it is prudent not to compromise, and owning a pair of quality shoes or boots may cost a little more, but if they look good and feel great, they can boost your image, as well as help with your posture and confidence.

As well as key pieces, there are several basics that can be replaced at very little expense, either each season or when they begin to wear out. You will need them for your general day-to-day wardrobe and they should be the starting point to which you add, building a diverse, fashionable yet modestly priced wardrobe. In addition, you should own items that stay in pristine condition for use solely on jobs. For example, boys need a pair of unbranded canvas trainers and a pair of smart shoes as these are often requested for shoots and shows. Similarly, girls should have a pair of heels that they are not too precious about sharing, as models often need to switch footwear on jobs.

The market in a certain location will enable a model to second-guess the kind of clothing required, as fashion

I know a model who …

went into a casting in a lovely dress. When the casting director asked her where she bought it from, she replied that she had stolen it from a shoot. The casting director did not look impressed!

Must-Have Shopping List

GIRLS

Underwear

Nude, seamless G-string

Nude and black bras: strapless, T-shirt (smooth cups, no lace), sports and push-up

Good-quality matching lingerie set

One flattering bikini

Casual wear

Dark blue and black skinny jeans

Black leggings and opaque tights

A basic selection of white, black and grey vests and T-shirts

One feminine summer dress with movement in the skirt

Formal wear

One plain black evening dress to the knee or just above

A white shirt

Black fitted suit – trousers or black pencil skirt to the knee

A selection of accessories: earrings, necklaces, bracelets, etc.

Sportswear

One set of running or gym attire: crop top or tight gym vest with either shorts or leggings

Footwear

Various inexpensive heels in black and brown/tan – not too high

Trainers, pumps, boots

Wedges

Running shoes

BOYS

Underwear

Tight-fitting briefs

Tight-fitting boxers

Swimming trunks

Casual wear

Blue and black jeans (vary the fit to suit your physique)

Range of printed and plain well-fitting T-shirts

Casual shirts and polo shirts

Casual belts in black and brown

Formal wear

Black or navy suit

Smart blazer

White shirts

Smart trousers/jeans

Sportswear

Gym vests, shorts, tracksuit

Footwear

Boots in black and brown

Unbranded canvas trainers

Sports trainers

Top Fashion Dos and Don'ts

Do

- Do invest in a key piece such as a handbag, overcoat or shoes to tie a look together and spend a little extra for a classic item that you know will last.

- Do mix textures to give an expensive feel.

- Do your research, read fashion magazines and look online at fashion blogs.

- Do keep it clean and chic with a crisp shirt or immaculate white vest.

- Do dress to show off your best assets.

- Do buy things that go with at least two other things you already own.

- Do dress for the occasion.

- Do use accessories to embellish a simple outfit.

- Do wear what you choose with confidence.

- Do experiment at home.

Don't

- Don't feel you must buy designer clothes to be fashion forward.

- Don't wear more than two trends together if possible.

- Don't fall victim to the whims of fashion, especially if they don't suit you.

- Don't wear too many patterns at one time.

- Don't wear anything too tight, too sexy or too see-through.

- Don't wear old, tired clothes.

- Don't aim to look like you've just stepped off the runway. Less is more.

- Don't over-accessorize.

- Don't let fashion swamp you. It should enhance you, not hide you.

- Don't try too hard.

differs within various countries. If you are planning on working in a hot, beachside country for example, expand your clothing essentials accordingly. Consider denim and black shorts, soft feminine skirts, a wider selection of bikinis, flip-flops and so on. Warmer climates often mean a more relaxed dress code.

A MODEL'S MUST-HAVE SHOPPING LIST

These basics mixed in with personal items will give a model the chance to show his or her style along with ensuring they are prepared to supply specific items for a shoot or casting. The table opposite lists the items a model is expected to have to hand.

THE HIDDEN COST

It is well documented that some clothing brands have, in the past, been guilty of using factories in less-developed countries that employ unethical labour practices. As consumers, we have a collective responsibility to ask questions about how and where clothing is made and to ensure that the bargains found on the high street do not come at a hidden cost. Research the brands you buy and if you are not satisfied that the workers are getting a fair deal or feel that children are being exploited, don't hand your money over. This is the most powerful statement you can make because without a demand, the need for supply dwindles and if enough people speak up, then even the largest multinationals will be forced to listen.

In summary, how you chose to dress is a very personal decision and most people want their clothing to suit their personality, style and look. However, like many other professionals, going to work means wearing a uniform or dressing in a particular way and this is no different for models. On days when you are casting, it will significantly improve your chances of booking work if

Take care of yourself, be healthy, and always believe you can be successful in anything you truly want.

Alessandra Ambrosio

you shape your image in the direction the client has either specified or might expect. Furthermore, consider how the clothes will appear on camera as you may be photographed or filmed. For example, try to avoid stripes, especially for television commercial castings, as they don't translate well on screen.

Neutrality and subtlety are key, so remember not to overdo a trend. Often the looks showcased in fashion magazines are for maximum photographic impact and may not translate well for you on a day-to-day basis. Also remember that trends can go out of fashion almost as soon as they arrive, so try not to base your core style on the season's look. Classic and clean styles that highlight your best features are a great place to start. From there, you can cleverly accessorize even the simplest of looks to add a personal touch. With so many popular shops available on the high street, competition for your business means you don't have to break the bank to look good and, most of all, whatever your style, wear it with confidence.

Final Thoughts on . . . Your Look

Take responsibility for yourself because no one's going to take responsibility for you.

Tyra Banks

By combining good nutrition, exercise, skincare, haircare and clever styling and make-up application, you can present potential clients with a look that is layered, versatile and dynamic. However, eating too little, over-exercising and over-spending on products and clothes will only leave you unhappy, so be sure to employ moderation when honing your exterior. Lastly, as a final thought, remember that a good look is just the beginning and is the bare minimum for models. You also need to focus on your book and attitude.

3: Your Book

I like creating images.

Kate Moss

Over the course of a lifetime a person will have their photograph taken thousands of times and how these images turn out is usually of little consequence. However, if you hope to make a career from modelling, then being photogenic is essential. A good look alone is not enough and being physically attractive is not the same as being photogenic. There are plenty of people who are very good-looking in the flesh, yet the camera never seems to find that aspect of them. Equally, a model may have a special relationship with the lens that brings out a beauty not always seen by the naked eye. To be consistently successful, it is important to have both qualities. A good diet, plenty of exercise and the right skincare can help with your physical appearance. By learning how to translate a good look into fantastic photographs, you can build up a strong portfolio and even stronger client base. Finally, remember to treat every photo shoot as a showcase for future work. Preparation and professionalism are just as important as being photogenic.

HOW TO BE PHOTOGENIC

Being photogenic is neither art nor science; it's a combination of both. A photograph might appear to tick all the right boxes, but because photography is so subjective, the best shots will always invite the viewer to see further than the obvious. Photographic styles may differ, but there are four areas you need to consider in order to be consistently photogenic: the light, your face, your shape and the photographer. Think of these as the foundations for a house that are decorated by the shot's composition, location and styling.

THE LIGHT

Without light there is no photography. By using a combination of flashes and ambient light, a photographer can set the tone for an image's final outcome. Equally, it is the responsibility of the model to consider the light's composition when being photographed. Vary your relationship with the light on set. Use the angles, strength and type of light to alter the mood, hide or highlight different aspects of the clothing and to complement your features.

YOUR FACE

Getting to know your face might seem like an odd concept at first, but understanding how your features complement each other is essential. Study yourself in a mirror and pay attention to how the light reacts to your face from different angles and with varying expressions. Also try this in differently lit rooms and experiment with your make-up and hairstyle. As well as practising expressions in a mirror, try conveying different emotions with just your eyes. An accomplished model is able to affect the mood of an image drastically with the subtlest variations in eye movement. Ultimately, you might be surprised by what you find, and using this

Back-lit shots usually make for captivating and powerful imagery.

When shooting lingerie or underwear, use light and dark to exaggerate definition of muscle tone.

Use your eyes to convey emotion and you will need little else.

knowledge during a photo shoot will allow you to instantly find your mark without hesitancy or needing further direction.

When investigating various expressions, girls should try to find a happy medium between being sensual but not overtly sexual, strong but not unapproachable and sultry but not miserable. Similarly, boys often need to come across as urban but not threatening, masculine but not wooden and charismatic but not cheesy. Also, being too expressive doesn't make for an attractive image. For example, try to avoid creasing your forehead or furrowing your brow.

Over time, these skills will develop and you'll find a balance. The easiest way to find the correct expression is to understand the story being told in the photograph. Sometimes, it can be helpful to think of yourself as an actor playing a role and use the styling, hair, make-up and location as indicators to your character. By doing this, you can not only cast off any nerves and present a more confident version of yourself, but every expression will be a more genuine representation of the emotion you are trying to portray. Also, try using emotional memory recall – a trusted acting method that draws on past experiences – to add honesty to your performance. Emotional memory recall involves casting your mind back to significant moment in your life, but instead of remembering what *happened*, you try to remember the way you *felt*. For example, recalling the first time someone broke your heart can conjure up an array of emotions that, when relived, can bring honesty to the performance.

When looking at the camera, extend your field of vision by looking through the lens rather than at it. This adds depth to your expression and enhances your connection with the person viewing the image. This is particularly apparent in portrait photographs where the eyes dominate the shot. In contrast, looking away from the camera can make the audience feel like a casual observer. Overall, a simple change in eye line can put a completely different spin on an image, so always check with the photographer how much eye contact they want. As a starting point, spend about 80 per cent of your time looking directly into the camera.

Blinking is a natural response and during any photo shoot there are bound to be a couple of shots where the model's reflexes have got the better of them. However, blinking too much will waste time and can cause frustration, so if your eyes are tired or sore, then use some drops during the shoot. Strong sunlight can also cause a model's eyes to close involuntarily so ask the photographer for a countdown from three to one or, in extreme cases, request something black to be held up next to the camera to help prevent glare. The fraction of a second after you open your eyes can be enough to get the shot before the sunlight welds them shut again.

YOUR SHAPE

What you say with your body can be just as expressive as the sentiment portrayed by your face. When you are in

Use trial and error to perfect your expressions and the mood you are hoping to convey.

When you are modelling, you are creating a picture, a still life, perhaps something like a silent film. You convey emotion but you are only using your body.

Helena Christensen

front of a camera, try not to 'pose' in the traditional sense of the word. In fact, 'posing' is a term that should never apply to good models because consciously forcing a pose will leave a model looking unnatural, awkward or clichéd. Instead, think of what your body shape is offering the camera with regard to the feel and emotion of the photograph.

A great starting point for both boys and girls is to just be natural and imagine yourself standing at a bus stop or waiting for a train. Better still, the next time you are on a platform, take a second to examine your posture as well as those around you. Note how it feels to stand naturally: the spacing of your feet and your weight distribution, as well as the bends and curves of your arms and where you hands unconsciously rest. This will help you slip back into 'bus stop' mode easily, allowing for an unforced body shape. From this comfortable and neutral position you can begin to add changes and personal touches. Never be afraid to practise in front of a full-length mirror to better understand your body. Again, this may seem silly, but it will give you the confidence to express yourself on set and this is one of your greatest assets as a model.

Once you have a combination of postures and expressions, you can begin to combine the variations so that,

With each click of the camera, offer the photographer something else to work with. Don't be afraid to try something quirky, playful or outrageous.

The Light

- Take note of where each flash is.
- Never cast shadows over yourself.
- Choose your angles to change the mood.

Your Face

- Your eyes need to tell the story.
- Emotional memory recall.
- You don't always have to look to camera.

Your Shape

- If in doubt, be natural.
- Variation, variation, variation.
- Take your time and take a break.

The Photographer

- Review and discuss the photos.
- Communicate, listen and offer ideas.
- If you feel uncomfortable, then speak up.

Nude shots can be artistic and beautiful but require trust between photographer and model. If you feel unsure, then don't be pressured into shooting them.

with each click of the camera, you offer the photographer something slightly different. This could be as small as the direction of your eyeline, tilting your head or changing which hand is in a pocket. Alternatively, complete alterations in body shape, shifting your entire weight to the other foot or changing your angles can reinvigorate your posture. Never be afraid to ask for a few seconds to relax, shake out any rigidity and start again.

THE PHOTOGRAPHER

The tone in any photo shoot is determined by the photographer, making it fundamental to form a good understanding with the person behind the camera. The quality of this relationship will almost always affect the outcome of the final image. In many ways, the bond between model and photographer can be quite intimate, and in a noisy studio it can feel as though there is a silent and personal connection. The more relaxed and comfortable both parties feel in each other's

company, the easier the creative expression will be. As with any relationship, it is crucial to communicate clearly and even before the first shot is taken, you should take a few minutes to talk to the photographer about what they expect from you and what they hope to achieve in the shot. If there is a mood board, discuss the photographs but don't try to replicate the image exactly. Its presence is there to help the client better pass on their vision for the shoot.

During the shoot variation is very important, so try to alter what you are offering the camera with each new shot. Take your time and work at your own pace, the photographer will follow you. Quite often, the photographer will ask you to hold a particular look or posture as they alter the camera's angle.

From time to time, they may even offer direction about how to behave. Listen to what is being said, because whilst a good model requires little direction, you should always react accordingly when it is given. If you feel the photographer is not being vocal enough, then check whether you are on the right track and ask for some pointers. If the photographer is quiet, it is usually because you are doing a good job and they don't want to disturb your rhythm.

At the beginning of a shoot or after a change in the lighting or styling, most photographers like to take a few test shots and then review their work, using either the camera's digital display or on a nearby computer screen. Final checks are then made before the shoot begins in earnest. At this point, ask to see the shots, because by catching a glimpse of what the photographer is seeing through the viewfinder, you'll have a more complete understanding of how the final image will turn out. A word of warning though; a model who just wanders off set can cause frustration and resentment amongst the crew, especially if time and effort have been spent finding the perfect light or a particularly tricky item of clothing is finally looking good on camera. Never leave the set without asking permission first.

Finally, a photographer should never make you feel uncomfortable, self-conscious or unworthy. Being a photographer comes with a perceived position of power and, unfortunately, there are a very small minority who wield this in an inappropriate way. Promises or threats can force models, particularly younger ones, down a path they later regret. If you feel this at any time or on any shoot, then speak up. Talk to your agent, client or the offending photographer and politely explain your unease at the situation. Remember: no one controls your career path but you.

I know a model who ...

fell asleep in the middle of the room on a photo shoot. People had to step over him and, to this day, the client refuses to book him.

An image captured in a photo studio. Simple but effective.

PHOTO SHOOTS: LOCATIONS, STYLES AND CREW

Understanding how you are affected by light, mastering your facial expressions, employing a variety of shapes and communicating with the photographer are all essential. The next step to being consistently photogenic is to use these skills in various locations, over a wide variety of photographic styles, either singly or in groups and all with the same level of confidence.

LOCATION
The location of a shoot will greatly affect the final image. Various locations each present different challenges to the model, photographer and crew. The three types of location are: photographic studios, location houses and just about anywhere you can put a camera and model.

Location houses are comfortable, welcoming and often lavish.

Studios

The working area of photographic studios usually consists of a few flashes, reflector boards and a Colorama – a paper background. They can be situated in large purpose-built buildings able to cater for several shoots simultaneously or in a small room in the back of an office. Studio shoots afford the photographer complete control over their environment, allowing each element, including the model, to be set up and adjusted as needed.

The simplicity of studio shooting gives all concerned enough time and control to create the exact image required, but it does put pressure on the model to make the photograph more interesting. There is likely to be one main flash complemented by smaller lights and reflectors, so pay attention to your angles in reference to this.

Sometimes elaborate sets are created and lit in such a way that they appear to be glamorous locations. For example, a cold studio in Germany can be transformed in the photographs to appear as a scorching beach in Barbados. All that is needed is the right lighting, some clever post-production and, of course, a convincing model. Overall, a studio is a professional and safe environment to work in.

Location Houses

Working in a location house is very similar to shooting in a studio. The only real difference is the sets have already been created, which slightly reduces the photographer's level of control. For the model, the added scenery makes the whole process a little more theatrical and by

The warm glow of sunlight can cause squinting, but you only have to have your eyes open long enough to catch the shot.

Shooting in exotic locations is a fantastic way to earn money, but remember that you are there to earn money, not have a holiday.

embracing the interesting surroundings, it is easier to get into character.

Perhaps the only downside to location house shooting is the higher cost of the space compared with studios, and clients therefore increase the workload as they try to get more value for money. However, this should be of little concern to a well-prepared and professional model and location houses are a great place to work. Do a good job and you're likely to have some strong images for your portfolio in return.

Shooting Outside

Shooting outside is always a tricky prospect. The weather and ambient light constantly change, and in doing so, affect the final image. Also, there are factors such as the general public and temperature; these make no difference to the photograph but do affect the atmosphere on set. As far as the model is concerned, the issues

surrounding the photograph will always take priority. For example, being heckled by a group of builders whilst shooting underwear in winter is not fun. You will, nevertheless, be expected to perform with the same level of professionalism as you would in a comfortable, warm and closed set. Also, strong sunlight, particularly in hotter climates, can make even the best model squint, but it is always appreciated if you do your best, work with the photographer and open your eyes long enough to get the shot. However, the challenges presented by working in an environment where so many factors are

I know a model who ...

got so drunk on a trip that he urinated in his room mate's suitcase. For the rest of the trip he was treated like a total idiot.

uncontrollable are vastly outweighed by the benefits. Outdoor location shots are frequently the most dynamic. As a result, models are flown thousands of miles if the client has a specific location in mind.

Travelling to an exotic or extreme location is a genuine perk of the job. These productions usually pay well, the photographs add new dimensions to any portfolio and the trips are always memorable. Shoots usually start as the sun is rising, before its angle and strength are unfavourable. During the hours when the sun is too high, models are given free time to do anything from surf to snowboard depending on the location. This freedom comes with responsibility and it is important to remember that you are not on holiday. Take extra care not to get sunburned and if hours were spent on hair and make-up, then ensure the hard work is not undone. Also, shoots usually resume in the late afternoon and conclude at sunset, so always be prompt for the resumption of work. During the hours of free time, save your energy; days are often long.

Editorial shots are sometimes designed to challenge and elicit an unexpected response.

STYLE

Commercial photography in advertising uses a combination of style and substance to inform and entice the consumer. Different clients employ varying levels of art and function in their work depending on their intended audience, their advertising strategy and the current trends in the market. At one end of this spectrum are fashion editorials for magazines. The flip side is studio catalogue shoots, and somewhere in between the two is lifestyle photography. For working models there are pluses and minuses to each type of production. Factors such as day rates, creative freedom, photograph quality and career development make every photo shoot a chance for you to grow professionally.

Fashion Editorials

Editorial or high fashion photography is very artistic in its composition, giving both model and photographer room to express themselves. At its most extreme, editorial photography uses dramatic lighting, emotive locations, unconventional styling and greatly exaggerated hair and make-up to portray a type of hyper-realism that exists purely for aesthetic purposes. Within the scene, the model is free to act out their role using unconventional body shapes and quirky expressions to create an altogether more edgy and provocative image. With such freedom to push boundaries, and the playful nature of the styling and make-up, editorial shoots can be very creative, exhilarating and memorable places to be. The photographer is likely to be open to a free exchange of ideas and is usually happy for the model to feature heavily in the creative process. Allow yourself to offer personal touches.

There can, however, be a tendency for those involved to occasionally take shoot days a little too seriously. Models are rarely required to smile in the photographs and if a client or creative director suspects a model of mocking the artistic integrity of the shoot, they might get frustrated or even take offence. Also, most editorial shoots are normally put together on a shoestring budget, meaning the model is likely get paid very little, if at all. Instead, there is usually the promise of photographs for the model's portfolio. These images can be useful allies in your bid to secure more lucrative jobs. Even if during the shoot you feel the photos won't end

Shooting couples' photography can be a lot of fun with the right partner. Find chemistry and balance and enjoy the experience.

Couples modelling can be fun. Just approach it with respect, trust – and good oral hygiene!

up in your book, still treat this work with just as much honesty, enthusiasm and professionalism as paying work, because experience and a good reputation are more valuable than any tear sheet.

Lifestyle

Lifestyle photography in the marketplace is designed to appeal to the consumers' aspirations towards a 'better' life. Commonly, the themes include personal success, health, blossoming love, family contentment and the strong bonds of friendship. Sets and locations tend to be well lit, the hair and make-up natural and the mood of the photographs generally warm, friendly and approachable.

The images are filled with vibrancy, health, wealth and happiness, which means the models must exude these qualities for the consumer to believe the scene. Equally important is the need for there to be a chemistry between the models on set, especially when shooting couples. It can be quite strange meeting a person for the first time and then almost immediately having to look longingly into their eyes or even kiss. Sometimes you will be asked to hold an eyeline that appears in the photograph to be directly at the other model but in reality is not: an expression known as 'cheating the eyes'. Either way, it is crucial to show respect to your fellow model and trust that they will do the same. If possible, try to get to know them as best you can before shooting. Personal and oral hygiene are a must, not only as a courtesy to fellow models, but also for confidence. If you ever feel a model is acting inappropriately during a couples' shoot, then speak up as they may be unaware they have crossed the line. Shooting couples' photography can be a lot of fun with the right partner. Find chemistry and balance and enjoy the experience.

Group Photography

Group photographs are always the most difficult to set up because of the increased number of variables within the shot. The ambient light will affect models in different ways depending on their position, so try not to cast shadows on those around you whilst ensuring that you have enough light for yourself. Furthermore, the dynamic of group shots can be tricky as photographers strive for a natural but controlled shot. Too static and a photo will appear contrived, and too chaotic will make

for an aesthetically displeasing image. Invariably, group shots will take longer to perfect, so it is the responsibility of the models to be patient and maintain energy levels. An easily frustrated or difficult model can soon fall out of favour with the group, especially if their lack of professionalism is to blame for unnecessary delays.

Catalogue Photography

Catalogues offer consumers a comprehensive view of what is on sale, making this type of work lucrative and consistent, if a little repetitive. The key point to remember is that, in any catalogue, the focus of the shots has to be on the product first and the model second. Posture, expression and use of light all have to be geared towards presenting the garment in the most positive way possible. For example, a floaty dress is best complemented in a soft and feminine way. By contrast, something more structured requires a stronger stance. Take note of the product details such as branding, zips and design features and be careful not to cover, distort

The more elements in a shot, the harder it is to look natural, so be patient, professional and relaxed.

Making friends with your colleagues isn't essential, but it really helps.

or place these details in shade. Better still, offer the camera the areas you feel are unique to the garment.

Studio-based catalogue shoots usually revolve around the client hoping to shoot as many different clothes as possible, often making the pace of work quite frenetic. With such a high shot count, each outfit is given just a few minutes, pressuring both photographer and model to get what is needed in a relatively short amount of time. Subsequently, by the end of the day, the photographer could be in possession of thousands of images, making variation very important. Move with each click of the camera, giving the client as many different options as possible. It might help to use a basic repertoire of moves that you feel confident with and repeat this for each change of clothing. This will allow you to work quickly and efficiently, and give you the self-assurance to be more expressive once you feel the client has what they need.

The sheer volume of work and the repetitive nature of catalogue shoots can make for long days. Nevertheless, they are still fun places to be if you approach the work with an upbeat and positive mentality. Also, there are ways to reduce the workload by paying attention to your surroundings. For example, a photographer might not notice that a flashbulb has stopped working, and by bringing it to the attention of the team, the problem can be sorted without too much delay. Similarly, clothing with a mark or crease might need to be shot again if this is not noticed and talking to the stylist or subtly removing it will prevent extra work and a waste of time and energy.

I know a model who …

insisted that the same song be played on repeat for three hours during a photo shoot. She drove everyone crazy.

Online photography or web shoots are very similar to studio catalogue shoots. There are likely to be a lot of outfit changes, meaning the pace of work is, again, quite fast. One difference is that the photography is sometimes complemented by short videos of the model walking and turning in the clothes. This has increased over the last few years as companies have become more Internet aware and it is a great chance for them to showcase their clothing in real time. Speak to the photographer about how you should approach these short videos and, as always, let your personality shine.

Website photography can sometimes be unrecognisable, meaning that the final crop of the image will not include the model's face. Also be aware this type of work generally comes with a reduced day rate, but this doesn't mean you should approach website shoots with any less vigour or expression. On the plus side, unrecognisable work won't hinder your chances of securing work for competing brands.

Occasionally, when shooting catalogues, look books or websites, you may find that you are so efficient the work is completed well ahead of schedule. Then the next time you're booked, either the available time is reduced, along with your rate, or the workload is increased. Don't worry, as this is a reflection of the client's confidence in you and a sign that you will secure business from them time and time again.

After the shoot, try and get a copy of the catalogue you have worked for. Whilst these photographs usually won't be suitable for your portfolio, it is a good idea to examine which shots the client chose as the final image and to refine your repertoire accordingly for future shoots. Examples of work are also useful for visa considerations, because the more established you can show yourself to be, the easier it is when trying to attain access to a new market.

I know a model who ...

tries to be so friendly with clients on jobs that it looks like an act.

CREW

At their busiest, there can be a whole host of people from different professions at a photo shoot. Whilst each production is different, it is likely that during its early stages a client will entrust a creative director and photographer with their vision. Then, as the idea gains momentum, a producer is approached and given a brief, and they then use their resources, contacts and knowledge to form a team. Locations are sourced, stylists and make-up artists recruited, models are cast and, eventually, the jigsaw fits together in the hope that the final shoot day will be a fruitful and enjoyable place to work. Each member of the team has an important role to play in the success of the production, as well as the atmosphere on set. Post-shoot, the client will assess the production and if the photos and experience were positive, they may well decide to reunite the team for subsequent projects.

THE CLIENT

Over the course of a successful career, a model will work with hundreds of different clients, creative directors, advertising executives and producers, in various markets and on an array of projects. Some become regular faces, whilst others you may only meet once before moving on to the next shoot. Either way, you should always aim to leave the client with a positive and lasting impression about the quality of your work and the way you are perceived as a person. Above all, remember that there is a difference between being friendly with the client and being their friend. This is equally true for first-time and regular clients. It only takes one act of casual unprofessionalism to undo the good work done at a casting or on previous jobs.

When working for a client for the first time, remember to relax and be yourself. Your look, book and attitude at the casting persuaded someone to give you the job, and now is the chance to repay that goodwill with results. On arrival, at least one of the people on set will recognize you from your composite card or the casting, but re-introducing yourself is still important. It serves to let the client know that you have arrived and are in the right frame of mind to work.

Throughout the shoot day, whenever you are in

contact with the client, it is imperative to show a controlled enthusiasm for the project. Always speak of the product or clothing in a favourable manner and take up as little of the client's time as possible when you are not needed on set. Models who exhaust the client by being too boisterous rarely find themselves booked again. Equally, models who create a cold atmosphere on set will fail to make an enduring impact and apathy can be just as frustrating for clients and crew.

Whilst shooting, always communicate with the client and photographer to ensure they get what they need. Sometimes, this can be at the expense of you getting images for your book, but remember: a good model focuses on the photograph, not their ego. If the client wants to shoot the back of your head, for example, then it's their choice and you are being paid to be shot that way.

At the end of the day, let the client know how much you enjoyed the experience and express your gratitude for lunch, travel arrangements, accommodation or any effort the client exerted to make your time on the project less stressful. Further still, enthuse about seeing the final images and ask if and when they might be available to add to your portfolio. Some clients will offer you their business card to contact them at a later date or ask for your details in return. Try not to give these because it may send out an inappropriate signal. If a client needs to get hold of you, then your agent should always be their first port of call.

After the shoot send a short email again thanking the client and, if you are hoping to acquire the images for your book, then politely ask for a selection of images in whichever format best suits the photographer. These might not necessarily be the shots the client chooses for their final usage, but the client's needs and your portfolio's needs can be very different.

If a client likes your work and personality, then they may well book you again for future productions. Catalogues and web shoot clients are always on the lookout for models who look great in the shots and make shoot days enjoyable. However, even if a client books you consistently, it is important not to become complacent or behave casually when shooting. Regular clients will soon look elsewhere if a model's work or behaviour begins to slide. Treat every client, every time, with a high level of respect.

I know a model who ...

went home without changing out of the clothes and then didn't bring them back for the next day's shoot! The client and photographer were so annoyed they sent him home to get the clothes and then changed their mind, telling him not to come back.

MODELS

Whenever working with other models, it is always a nice idea to develop a relationship both on and off the set. This means more than just acting in a professional and courteous way, because of all the people on a photo shoot, they are likely to be the ones you spend the most time with. Photo shoots invariably require preparation, resulting in extended periods of down time. You can spend this reading, on your laptop or chatting on your mobile, but it is better to have a conversation with your fellow models. It shouldn't be too difficult to establish a rapport as you may have seen the other models at castings, around your agency or on previous jobs. Also, you may have more in common than you first realize; the client booked you because they felt that you would gel in the final image and on set. Once the ice is broken, you will feel more relaxed when the shooting starts and even if you don't end up shooting together, being sociable always makes shoot days more enjoyable.

There are some subjects that you should avoid discussing with your fellow models on a shoot. The most important area to avoid is money, and more specifically the rate for the job you are currently working on. Different agencies negotiate different rates for their models, and even within agencies, models can be paid varying amounts for a whole host of reasons. Therefore, discussing money with other models unquestionably results in one or both parties feeling resentful towards each other, their agent or the client. If a model does commit the cardinal sin of asking you about the basic studio fees or potential buyouts, then avoid the question, play dumb and hope they take the hint.

The models on set can sometimes come from different cultures, backgrounds and age groups, so be open-minded when meeting people for the first time. Also, try not to form judgements too quickly and if a model is seemingly unfriendly or hard to talk to, then always give them the benefit of the doubt. If you sense that someone would rather be left to their own devices, then give them space and divert your attention elsewhere. Eventually, they may come round and if they don't, then at least you tried.

This respect should continue whilst shooting and being generous to the other models in the shot will invariably lead to a better atmosphere. Obstructing their light or view of the camera will only mean more time is needed to get the desired outcome.

GROOMING TEAM

Hair and make-up artists are among the friendliest and most sociable people a model will meet. From the moment you sit down to have your hair or make-up done, you are usually greeted by a relaxed individual whose aim is to beautify you to best of their ability and shape your look in the direction of the client's brief. Help them by turning up to the shoot with a clean face and hair and a positive disposition. Before they begin, talk to them about the brief and notify them of any products your skin or scalp might react badly to.

Occasionally, a model might be unhappy with the final outcome and completely overhaul their own hair or make-up. This is not only an insult to a paid professional, but also an indirect swipe at the client. The client hired the hair and make-up team and it is up to them to decide if the quality of work is good enough to be photographed. If you do wish to make subtle changes, then be discreet and keep your thoughts to yourself.

During the shoot, good make-up artists and hairstylists will closely monitor the production and adjust the model's appearance accordingly. However, even the most dedicated of professionals can sometimes get pulled in different directions and if, for example, the hairstylist or make-up artist is working on another model whilst you are being photographed, then pay attention to your own grooming. If you get hot and feel this might be showing on camera, don't be afraid to ask for some tissue, powder and lip balm. Similarly, if you notice your hair falling out of place, don't wait for someone else to speak up and ask for the hairstylist's assistance.

STYLISTS

Fashion styling is a very creative profession and, in many ways, the colours of the clothing on a shoot are similar to those on the palette of an artist. Further still, the various styles and textures of each garment could be compared to differing brushstrokes employed to paint an even fuller picture.

More often than not, the styling will subtly complement the scenery as well as the model's skin tone and body shape, and while the result may appear effortless, the reality is that a great deal of thought goes into compiling outfits for a production. Liaising with the client, buying and cataloguing the clothes, then steaming, cleaning, repairing and returning the outfits make a stylist's job as pragmatic as it is creative.

Therefore, it helps to recognize the amount of time spent by the stylist by not adding to their workload. For example, when wearing a freshly ironed outfit, don't crease the clothing by immediately sitting down or folding your arms. Similarly, change out of the clothing during lunch and never take food or drink into the changing area. By showing the clothing a level of respect, you instantly gain appreciation from the stylist. Other ways to assist include checking whether a label needs removing. If it doesn't show and is not causing too much discomfort, then leave it be. Otherwise, ask the stylist to cut it out so as not to damage the garment. Also, be careful not to get make-up on the clothes when changing. This is polite to both the styling and grooming team and, in return, they will always assist you should you need it.

Frequently whilst shooting, the stylist may need to adjust the fit of the clothes with pins and clips. Assist them by remaining still as they make the changes and then find the intended body position for the next shot. Also, if you notice a problem with the garment, then bring it to the stylist's attention. However, this should be done with discretion as being overtly critical of the quality, style or fit of the clothing in front of the client is disrespectful and leads to resentment.

I know a model who ...

gets really defensive when given direction by the crew. She's very spiky.

Never be tempted to steal any items of clothing from the stylist or client. Photographic samples are often unique and, due to the importance of these garments, they are carefully monitored. Alternatively, the clothing on set might be from the stylist's personal collection or has to be returned to the high street. Either way, theft is extremely rude and rarely goes unnoticed. The most likely outcome is that the offending model is never booked again and their reputation is severely tarnished. If an item of clothing catches your eye, then speak to the stylist or the client about its availability at the end of the day. They may sell you the clothing at a heavily discounted rate or take your details and send you the item once it is no longer needed. Make a really positive impact and, under the right circumstances, the stylist might offer you the clothing as a gift. Whatever happens, be grateful and recognize their kind gesture with a follow-up card or email.

PHOTOGRAPHY TEAM

With so many variables on a photo shoot, it is not surprising that a photographer needs some help, particularly on larger productions. Photographers' assistants, therefore, act as additional pairs of hands and eyes on set. Also, advances in camera and computer technology often require the presence of a specialist digital assistant or retoucher. An image can be manipulated so that, in a matter of minutes, the photographer, client and model will know how the finished photograph will look.

Both photographic and digital assistants work very hard and always seem to be busy. As they hurriedly shift equipment, change backgrounds, measure and adjust the lighting, put down markers and make tea, it can be easy to overlook how important they are. Nevertheless, always be mindful that a photographer often has a close-knit group with whom they work repeatedly, making your behaviour towards every member of that team just as important. Furthermore, today's assistant is

I know a model who ...

often reapplies her own make-up on shoots. What's more is she's really blatant about it and does it right in front of the make-up artist.

I know a model who ...

stole a sample thinking she would get away with it. The stylist realized what had happened and called her agent. She had to give back the clothing, lost the client and her agent was so annoyed they cancelled her contract.

tomorrow's photographer and a good impression could open doors later in your career.

In summary, on every photo shoot there are a variety of people present from all walks of life with different personalities, skills and opinions. However, for the duration of their time together, they must combine to produce the best work possible and by focusing on this common interest, you can ensure a positive response and a good reputation. From time to time you might find you don't gel with a member of the team or the shoot isn't going as smoothly as planned, but always keep your views to yourself. You never know whom you're confiding in or who might be listening. Instead, save your energy for the shoot and display humour, humility and honesty on every occasion.

PREPARATION

One of the most exciting aspects about working as a model is that no two photo shoots are the same. However, there are enough similarities between jobs to allow you to prepare correctly and, in doing so, make the day much more enjoyable. More importantly, proper preparation acts as a courtesy to the team by saving time and energy, which in turn helps to create a positive atmosphere on set and enhance your status as a professional. Certain aspects of your preparation are made easier as often a list of specific requirements about grooming or styling is handed to your agent. There are also the basics, like personal and oral hygiene. In addition to these, there are crucial ways to prepare with respect to your face, hair, body, clothing and general comfort. These simple considerations could make the difference between you being rebooked or not.

Although the exact schedule depends on the workload and location, most shoot days follow a similar pattern.

Arrive	9.00 – 9.30
Hair, make up and styling	9.30 – 11.00
Shoot	11.00 – 13.00
Lunch	13.00 – 14.00
Shoot	14.00 – 17.00
Wrap	17.00 – 18.00

FACE

Always arrive with a clean, moisturized face. This allows the make-up artist to start work almost immediately without the need to scrape off any eyeshadow, lipstick or foundation. A moisturizer with a high SPF is useful if shooting outside, even if the sun doesn't appear to be particularly strong. For guys, the client will usually give an indication about stubble growth. If this information is unavailable or they wish to make a decision on facial hair length on the day, then be sure to take a beard trimmer and shaving kit. The hairstylist or make-up artist may well have grooming equipment, but this could run contrary to personal preference, so it is better not to rely on them.

HAIR

Wherever possible, a model's hair should always be the same cut and colour as it was the day of the casting. Sometimes, a shoot or show earlier in the week or even the previous day might require a slightly different colour, length or style. However, before your hairstyle changes, check with your agent that the client is happy to still book you and then send updated polaroids to avoid any problems, shocks or disappointment on arrival. Regardless of style, to save time, hair should always be clean, dry and product-free. Any waxes, gels or clip-in hair extensions you regularly use should be taken to the shoot and discussed with the hairstylist. This is appreciated, but do not be offended if they decide not to use them.

BODY

Daily body maintenance is essential for any model and it is particularly important the night or morning before a photo shoot. Fingernails and toenails should be natural, trimmed and clean. A layer of clear nail varnish is recommended for the girls. Also, for girls, armpits, legs and bikini lines should be smooth and hair-free. For boys, body hair needs consideration but differs depending on your look.

Be prepared to remove piercings, and if you have tattoos that you think the client would prefer not to have in the photograph, then bring cover-ups or body make-up.

The crucial point about body maintenance before a shoot is that you can never predict the styling or situations you might find yourself in. On a winter wear shoot, for example, you could wrapped up in hats, coats and gloves, with not a spare inch of flesh showing. Nonetheless, preparing for all eventualities will avoid any potential embarrassment or self-consciousness.

CLOTHES

Unlike most jobs, the clothes a model wears to work are rarely the clothes they end up wearing all day. However, careful consideration still needs to go into your attire as it may affect both the image and your comfort during the shoot. Underwear should always be seamless, neutral or flesh-coloured and unbranded. For boys, briefs preferably need to be quite tight to avoid showing up under clothes and girls should bring a strapless bra as well as a T-shirt bra. A spare pair of socks or tights is also recommended.

Footwear is another area to consider, because if the shoes don't fit a model, they will still be expected to squeeze into them. Sample shoe sizes in the UK are 7–8 for girls and 8–10 for boys. If your feet are out of this size range, then always take appropriate shoes to the shoot as an alternative. Also, when girls shoot lingerie or swimwear, a pair of high heels make their legs appear leaner and more toned. Sometimes the client will provide them, but, just in case, you should pack your own.

Prior to shooting you may receive a phone call from the stylist about bringing a few items of clothing to help out. Alternatively, a clothing brief that amounts to an entire suitcase full of garments can be handed to your agent. In either case, prepare and pack the items you intend to take the night before in order to avoid rushing in the morning and always be mindful of the condition, pattern and colour of the clothes. Visible branding should also be considered when raiding your wardrobe for garments to take with you and try not to take offence if the clothes aren't used. Offering the stylist additional options is a professional courtesy and ensures there is clothing present that definitely fits you.

GENERAL COMFORT

As well as the basics, such as hunger and thirst, you should also consider other factors like punctuality and boredom. After all, looking after yourself on a shoot, both physically and mentally, will increase your enjoyment of the job. This, in turn, is directly reflected in the quality of your work and the relationships you form on set.

Preparation for your general comfort begins the night before a shoot with punctuality planning. Being late is unprofessional and stressful but easily avoided by locating the desired destination on a map, calculating how long the journey will take and then planning to arrive ten or fifteen minutes early. If using public transport, then double-check for any scheduled disruptions to the service. Similarly, if you decide to drive, check for roadworks and remember to leave extra time for parking and travelling during the rush hour. You can even call the studio the day before for information about the cost and availability of parking in the area or if they offer reservable off-street parking.

As well as planning to be punctual, be sure to eat breakfast before you arrive and consider taking your own lunch, or at the very least some healthy snacks or meal replacement bars. Photo shoots tend to be littered with baked goods, chocolate bars, crisps and fizzy drinks. A model who doesn't prepare properly will find they either have to incorporate these into their diet or go hungry.

I know a model who ...

always asks everyone else how much they are getting paid for the job. It's so embarrassing because, most of the time, they're getting less than the rest of us!

This isn't a problem once in a while, but the more successful you become, the more often this dilemma could occur. If the client provides you with a healthy and nutritious lunch, you can save your food for dinner. Also stay hydrated by taking plenty of water.

As well as looking after your dietary needs, skincare is also important on shoots. Make-up wipes, cleansers and moisturizers all vary in scent, strength and the way they react to your skin. Therefore, fill a toiletry bag with these as well as deodorant, toothpaste, a toothbrush, lip balm or a neutral gloss, tweezers, a foundation and concealer. Sunblock is useful regardless of the time of year, as are umbrellas. Check the weather forecast for both the start and end of the day. Dress accordingly and never underestimate the variability of the weather conditions despite the season.

On most photo shoots there are often long periods when the model is not required on set and, in order to quietly enjoy this time, take a book, magazine, laptop or anything else that will prevent boredom or restlessness. Remember that other members of the production will be hard at work and a model complaining about being bored or one who requires constant attention is viewed as childish and draining. Leave valuable items, such as watches, rings and other jewellery, at home unless the stylist has requested specific items for the shoot. Maximize your impact by using your energy to create great photos and impress the crew.

One item that should never be left at home is your portfolio. Every job should be treated as a casting for a future job and although the client may have seen your book before, the photographer, make-up artist or stylist might be interested. In addition, if the shoot finishes earlier than expected, you can contact your agent about any other castings you could attend. At the very least, always have a few spare composite cards with you.

In summary, there are numerous clichés about preparation, such as 'fail to prepare, and you prepare to fail', and whilst the distinctions between success and failure for professional models are less clear-cut, correct preparation can only help. Arrive at every photo shoot thinking of it as a blank canvas to allow the styling and grooming team to mould you as the client desires. Refine your preparation with experience to suit locations, seasons and personal needs.

I know a model who …

always begs the stylist for free clothes and refuses to drop the subject if they are refused. Not cool.

PROMOTIONAL MATERIAL

Your card, portfolio, polaroids, web pages and other promotional materials are all vital tools in your bid to attract consistent, well-paid work. By ensuring that all are current and reflect your look in the best possible way, you can expand your appeal and access to clients considerably.

YOUR CARD

Composite cards, model cards or Z-cards as they are also called, are designed to promote a model with a high-impact snapshot of their career, abilities and pedigree. Although they can differ from agency to agency, they mostly follow a similar pattern. The front of a card shows the model's main picture, which is usually mirrored on

Your card should always be by your side. Remember: every card costs money, so treat them with care.

I know a model who ...

doesn't bring their own food to jobs and then complains about what they're given to the client.

the agency website and in the opening page of their portfolio. The model's name or stage name and their agent also feature. The back of a card displays several photographs and aims to show a range of angles and prestigious campaigns, and usually includes at least one shot of the model's body. It also displays measurements and agency contact details.

A good card is vital and should display a striking or beautiful image likely to catch the attention of clients you are hoping to attract. Head shots are commonly used on the front, whereas on the reverse a series of images displaying versatility and individualism that are bursting with personality are preferred. Whichever images you and your agent choose to grace your card, they must look like you. This sounds bizarre, but so often boys and girls are requested to castings based on their card and then arrive with different hair colours, styles, facial hair and body shapes, thus disappointing the client and wasting everyone's time. Also, after a busy casting, when

a client has a table full of cards before them, being able to put a card to a face will help recapture their eye, shifting you to the top of the heap.

Similarly, the measurements on your card need to be current and accurate. Everyone's body naturally changes over time and even at different points in the year, which is fine, as long as your agent is notified and your card updated accordingly.

Cards can be changed as often as you like, although if a particular photograph on the front seems to be generating a higher frequency of request castings or direct bookings, then consider leaving it for as long as possible. However, after six to eight months all cards should be updated in keeping with seasons and trends in the markets. Some models like to have a variety of cards for use with different clients depending on how editorial or commercial that client is perceived to be.

When deciding to change your card, think objectively about the elements of your previous card that captivated potential clients and casting directors alike. Schedule an afternoon with your agent and carefully look at which photographs work best as the main picture as well as various combinations for the back. Check your measurements and then print off a maximum of fifty copies as a trial run.

Just as businessmen and women carry their card with

A portfolio should open with a head shot. It's a great way to introduce yourself.

them at all times, so should you. Whenever you work, socialize and travel abroad, always keep at least one or two cards in your possession. This isn't idle vanity, because you never know whom you might meet. Photographers, show producers, casting directors and booking agents from foreign markets are everywhere and having your card with you might help you seize an opportunity others would miss. Finally, never run out of cards and if you notice there are only a couple left in your possession, head to your agency as soon as possible and pick up some new ones. It might be prudent to have a few at home that you keep separately from your book to ensure you never attend a casting without a card.

YOUR PORTFOLIO

At its most basic level, a portfolio, or book as it is also known, is a model's photographic résumé. As well as your personal portfolio, your agency will have a second book that can be sent to clients. Like any good CV, your personal and second books should include more than just examples of your work and should offer a real insight into the type of model, and person, you are. A strong, flowing and versatile portfolio can take a while to form, so be patient. However, with investment, initiative and persistence, you can build your book considerably faster and ensure that, before too long, the photographs within showcase you in the best possible light.

Most of all, it is important to avoid getting caught in a vicious circle of not securing good work because of a weak book and yet never improving the book through lack of work. Even with a steady stream of work, weeks or even months can go by before the shots find themselves in your book, making it crucial to always contact clients about image recovery. This is also known as chasing photographs, and whilst some view this as an agent's responsibility, it is your career, so take the initiative. This is especially relevant when the photographs are likely to add depth, dimension or prestige to your portfolio or for foreign markets' visa requirements.

Whenever dealing with clients, past, present and future, there are always unwritten codes of practice that should be followed. After all, speedy recovery of shots should not come at the expense of repeat business. Firstly, consider that a photographer can have literally thousands of images that need to be edited, retouched

and prepared for the marketplace and by asking the photography team about their intended post-shoot timetable on the day of the job, you can avoid pestering them too soon about the finished article. Similarly, speak to the client about their workload and proposed release

Top Tips for Tests!

- **Never sign a model release form on a test:** the images created should be for the sole purpose of improving your and the photographer's portfolios, and if they are to be used commercially, then you should be compensated appropriately.

- **Always notify your agent about the test:** by talking to your booker about the proposed photographer and their ideas, they can advise you accordingly.

- **Never shoot anything you cannot use:** free tests are a give-and-take between the photographer and model, but you should always find at least one scenario you are confident, if executed correctly, will bolster your book. Experimental and highly editorial shots should be balanced with more mainstream imagery depending on your look, career path and book requirements. Before a shoot agree the styling and story for the shoot and make sure this is adhered to.

- **Stop immediately if you feel pressured:** photographers can occasionally push boundaries on tests, which they might not normally do, especially with regards to full or partial nudity. Furthermore, models can feel pressured, or get caught up in the moment, and shoot something they later regret. In defence of photographers this is rare, but nevertheless, if you do not want images that are sexually explicit to make it into your book and if it is suggested that you remove your clothes, then stop the shoot immediately. Ask the photographer to explain their reasons and contact your agent for advice. The break in shooting should act as a chance for you to organize your thoughts and as a message to the photographer that you will not be bullied. Testing should be mutually beneficial and not an excuse for a photographer to exploit the model.

dates. Ask whether it would be possible for them to send tear sheets to your agency and who would be the best person to contact.

In the days after the shoot, send a follow-up email to the client and remember to always thank them in advance. As well as being a very low-pressure way of highlighting your desire to use the photographs as soon as possible, you can also reassure the client that the images are strictly for your book. Some clients worry that models will display their work on personal web pages or social networking sites before they have had a chance to release the images.

The client will usually respond promptly and in due course the photographs will arrive at your agency. However, if you have not received the tears after the agreed time, then send a polite email again requesting the work, and if you are unsuccessful after a third attempt, or if you have not even had a response, then

ask your agent to try on your behalf. Your booker will have dealt with the client previously and may have direct access to the person responsible.

Alternatively, request a CD-ROM from the photographer containing a selection of high-resolution images. This can be obtained faster than tear sheets and offers you and your agent a wider variety of shots to choose from. The downside is that these images are unlikely to be branded and may not be seen as an example of work. Therefore, it is best to acquire both hard and digital copies and build your book accordingly.

Overall, clients and photographers should send the finished article without the need for further prompting, but in practice this is not always the case. This can be frustrating because until the shots are in your book, on your card or on the agency website, potential clients will be unaware of new developments in your career. By helping your booker, you can not only retrieve photo-

Finding a good photographer and location is always a great excuse to create beautiful imagery that adds depth and dimension to your portfolio.

graphs faster, but also allow them to concentrate on finding you work.

TEST PHOTOGRAPHY

Test photography is a simple way to build your book, although you should not expect to fill your portfolio with one test. Every photographer has unique equipment and an individual style that, if overused, will be to your book's detriment. A good test should, therefore, yield a maximum of three pictures depending on the stage your career is at. Even established books can benefit from a new test from time to time, as it presents an opportunity to experiment with light, location, styling, posture, emotion, expression and just about every element of a photograph. The finished images can add substance and variation to any book as well a chance to work with a range of photographers.

As with every photo shoot, careful preparation is key. The first step is to know what is needed to strengthen

I know a model whose ...

portfolio is in tatters. Clients always complain they can't see her photos. Seems like a shame.

your book, and by speaking to your agent you can determine whether to arrange a 'paid test' or a 'free test'.

Paid Test

Paid tests can be arranged almost immediately and basically involve a model hiring a photographer to shoot and process the pictures for a fee. This fee depends on several factors including the perceived expertise of the photographer, the amount of time required for retouching, studio costs, their equipment and whether you wish them to print the shots. Like any purchase, it is best to shop around before deciding on one photographer, so

A well-received head shot can make a massive difference and is something to strive for.

ask your agent to recommend a few that you can research. Every photographer hoping to charge models for their services should have a website which displays their work. Look for range, styling, use of colour and whether they tend to specialize in shooting boys or girls. Above all, consider whether you want a particular photographer's work in your portfolio, and remember that it doesn't require a trained eye to know if you like a particular photographer's pictures. Also look at other models' books and cards to find ideas or compositions you like. Ask them about particular shots, whether they were tests and who photographed them. If they were paid tests, then find out the price, the photographer's personality and the speed at which they delivered the pictures.

Once you have contacted the photographer, speak to them about what you specifically require and how they propose to meet those needs. It might be an idea to meet in person, show them your portfolio and honestly discuss how it could be improved. If you recognize the photographer's thoughts or they seem to have limited

suggestions, it may be because you are dealing with a test photographer who recycles the same idea with a host of different models. This is not likely to be beneficial given that uniqueness is a key characteristic for both your book and for you as a model.

Other points to raise include the photographer's availability and whether they provide hair, make-up and styling. It is also wise to enquire about the level of post-production, the cost of prints and their overall fee. Paid tests require an initial fee, but from your research online, conversations with the photographer and the advice of your agent, you should have a fair indication whether these costs represent value for money. Ultimately, if you book countless jobs on the strength of one photograph, then your investment will be repaid many times over. Even so, never be afraid to negotiate and always stipulate that you will not pay the money until you receive the photographs. If the photographer refuses, then politely explain you cannot proceed. In fact, if you feel unsatisfied with anything, then don't feel obliged to continue, even if you, or your agent, have already agreed to the shoot.

On the shoot itself, take charge and if a photographer deviates from the initially discussed plan, then steer them back on course. Alternatively, they may be having a flash of inspiration and if you feel happy to hand them the reins, then feel free. The beauty of digital photography is that the images are instantly available, making it apparent whether the test is achieving its goals. Above all else, remember it's your money, so it's your time. Don't feel rushed, use the opportunity to its fullest and don't stop until you are completely satisfied.

Free Test

The alternative to a paid test is a free test. This involves models, photographers and sometimes even stylists, hairstylists and make-up artists all coming together to offer their expertise to create images for the benefit of their respective portfolios. As a model, you are neither being paid nor having to pay, but this doesn't mean you should test with just anyone. If a photographer approaches you or your agent about testing, you should still research them in the way you would for a paid test. Your time and your image are both precious commodities and if a photographer appears unprofessional or if

Top Tips for Your Promotional Material!

- Make sure you have both digital and hard copies of all your photographs. As well as your book, keep a 10GB flash drive with you whenever you go to castings, jobs or on trips.

- Your agency website and second book are just as important as your principal portfolio, so update all of them regularly.

- Throughout your book mix test photography with examples of work to show that you are versatile and in high demand.

- Keep all your photography safe. You never know when a potential client might describe a particular shot that you know you have in your back catalogue. Showing it to them might just get you the booking.

- If you don't like a photograph in your book, then take it out. Confidence in your book is key.

you feel their standard of work will not aid your portfolio or career, then respectfully decline. Furthermore, there are some rules that should never be broken under any circumstances.

COMPILING YOUR BOOK

Once you have a few tests and examples of work at your disposal, you should think about the structure and flow of your book. Compiling the photographs for maximum impact with potential clients is no easy task and, to begin with, it is better to rely on the experienced eye of your agent. They will have seen countless portfolios and understand the strength of your photographs, as well as the best way to showcase your look and personality. However, whilst your agent may have a highly informed opinion, photography is extremely subjective and it soon becomes clear that the response of others towards your book on castings is what really matters. In addition, taking control of your book offers a sense of achievement and independence and should boost your enthusiasm for your career. It also reflects positively on the way you relate to your book during castings, because pride in your portfolio is as vital as the photographs within.

Also in castings, gauge the response of others towards your book by listening for direct, or indirect, compliments, and always take note of the photographs that command a little more attention than others. Be brave and ask the opinions of as many different people in the business as possible. You can even canvas the thoughts of family and friends about their preferences. After all, they will know you implicitly and have the honesty to tell you if a photograph works. Over time, you'll have a fuller understanding about which photographs flatter, possess uniqueness or hold a level of prestige, as well as which colours, styles and moods belong together. The goal is then to feel confident enough to experiment with different combinations, and eliciting a positive reaction is both a science and an art form. For example, established psychological phenomena like primacy and recency effects mean that people have better memory for the first and last items in a list. Therefore, to make a lasting impression, you should place your high-impact photographs at start and close of your book.

Perhaps the best way to make an impact is if potential clients are greeted by a captivating head shot as they open the portfolio. This acts as an introduction and, whilst this might not be the most glamorous, edgy or progressive shot in your book, it is a true representation. Eye contact is recommended, and overall an initial head shot should deliver a feeling of health, self-assurance and contentment.

From there, just like a good novel, your book should tell a coherent story, consisting of a beginning, middle and end. Use chapters of varying mood, shade, colour and dimension and allow the viewer to catch a glimmer of your personality in each turn of the page. Be sure to include lingerie or underwear shots, casual and formal clothing, group shots, smiles, eyewear, beachwear and couples shots, and don't forget to use both black-and-white and colour imagery.

Length and versatility need to be finely balanced and, as your catalogue of tears and tests builds up, you'll have to omit certain photographs from your book. This may be hard at first, as you hope to display the full extent of your modelling talents, but having a few strong pictures will present a sharper, more focused image. Remember: quality, not quantity.

Equally important is the need to know the type of client whose attention you are hoping to gain. High fashion models are unlikely to be booked for lifestyle and catalogue work and if 90 per cent of your book is very commercial, then an overly edgy editorial might look out of place. Nonetheless, some editorial work will add variation.

Of course, the major benefit of a portfolio is that photographs can slide in and out with relative ease, making nothing permanent. With research, honesty and a bit of trial and error, you can adapt your book for the market, time of year, seasonal trends or even for individual clients, always ensuring it provokes the best response. A frequently overlooked area is a model's second book, so always ensure new tear sheets or

I know a model who ...

was really rude to a photographer's assistant. Years later, when the assistant was a famous photographer, he refused to work with that model and urged others not to work with her either.

images are scanned and added to your second book accordingly.

Finally, as well as the visual imagery your book offers, remember that every single photograph is accompanied by a unique anecdote, that when shared shows clients that you are great to work with. This is especially apparent for new faces because, with only a handful of photographs to choose from and a book that is not yet as strong as it could be, more emphasis falls on a model's look and attitude. For example, remembering the photographer's name and using it when discussing your book can make a notable difference. This isn't about name-dropping but showing that you are good with people and have an enthusiasm for your work.

I know a model who …

had her images stolen from her website and used by a stranger pretending to be her on a dating page.

YOUR WEBSITE

As your career develops, and particularly if you have several agencies dotted around the globe, you may want to have one web page dedicated solely to you. On this site you can showcase your most current and best photographic work in any way you choose. Also include video biographies, snippets from runway shows, your presenting and television commercial showreel, and links to your various agencies. If done well, this content can be a useful tool and reference point, especially when networking. However, without taking the right precautions, you leave yourself exposed both professionally and personally, so never reveal your personal phone number, address or even email address. If a photographer or client likes the work presented on the site, they should be able to contact your agent in order to secure your services. Also, websites should not be a way of avoiding the correct channels or trying to book commercial work without the knowledge of your agent. Model agencies exist to protect you from being exploited and if you have ever doubted this, then listen to your bookers whilst they negotiate day rates and usage for jobs. Remember: you and your agent are on the same side.

In addition, the photographs you put up on the site

I love photo sessions. I'm alone, I'm the queen, everyone's taking care of me.

Eva Herzigova

should be proofed against someone potentially downloading your entire portfolio and using it for their own purposes. Use low-resolution imagery and try to upload it with software that prevents easy access. For this reason, never put your professional shots on social networking sites. As well as blurring the distinction between your personal and private life, it dilutes the impact of your imagery and cheapens your brand exclusivity.

Lastly, designing and building a web page is a professional investment and not just a vanity project. The cost of its design and upkeep should be as low as possible if you are to maximize your profits from its creation. One way to minimize cost is to buy the domain name, hosting space and html software editor and design the page yourself. This option really depends on your technical abilities and the projected complexity of the site, but you may be surprised at how straightforward web design is once you familiarize yourself with the basics.

YOUR POLAROIDS

Originally, the term 'polaroid' applied to instantly developed photographs that were used to test the light and composition of a shot. Of course, today's digital photography has superseded this technology and what the industry now calls a 'polaroid' is a current snapshot of a model's true likeness. To begin with as a new face, the polaroids you take when you first join an agency could be the only record of what you look like for potential clients, making it really important to get these right. A full set of polaroids includes various head shots, body shots, profiles and maybe even a short video of you moving, walking and introducing yourself. Therefore, on the day your agency invites you in to take these shots, make sure you are properly prepared with a good night's sleep and that your body is looking as good as possible. Always wear clean, flattering underwear and take a bikini or swimming trunks just in case. Make-up application and hairstyling should be minimal and natural, respectively. As a rule, girls are best advised to wear something figure-hugging and neutral; a white vest, for example. Remember: polaroids are meant to show you, not what you're wearing. Similar neutrality should be applied to a male model's choice of clothing.

From there on you should periodically update your polaroids – and this doesn't always have to be at the agency. Find a friend, partner or family member to take the shots and, as long as it is someone you feel comfortable with who understands the basics of a camera, you can take polaroids anywhere. Use natural light whenever possible to ensure the polaroids depict your current state. You can even use a tripod and take your own polaroids once every few months, ready to send to your agent as and when they need them. For example, foreign market clients might ask for up-to-date shots as they are unable to see you in person. Unless the client has specifically indicated what your look should be and what you should wear, this catalogue of basic digital images could help.

If you are asked unexpectedly to have polaroids taken and you feel it really would be better to take them after some personal preparation, then ask your agent to wait a day or two. Unless it is urgent, your agent will agree, as it is better wait for stronger images.

Final Thoughts on . . . Your Book

I find modelling similar to dancing. Both help me learn to have a presence in front of people and are about poise and being patient.

Coco Rocha

Being photogenic is essential for a model, but having your photograph taken isn't as simple as standing on your mark and looking to camera. Your personality should be evident in every shot, and even when shooting in a bare studio with little frame of reference, your eyes, expression and shape should tell a story. The relationship you develop with a photographer, client and crew on set can make a real difference to an image's outcome, but you should never feel afraid to voice your opinion if you feel uncomfortable with direction or the projected outcome. Once you have some quality images at your disposal and your promotional material develops, you and your agent can adjust your career path accordingly, but remember that your look and book are useless without an attitude that surpasses them.

4: Your Attitude

Elegance is a question of personality, more than one's clothing.

Jean-Paul Gaultier

A positive attitude is vital to your success and one of the biggest differences between struggling and successful models is the understanding that whilst a good look and strong book are important, they only represent two parts of the puzzle. In fact, it's more accurate to say that these can't be achieved without a good attitude. For example, exercise routines and healthy eating are easy to discuss but, on a day-to-day basis, require focus and discipline. Similarly, the levels of energy and expression a model brings to a shoot will always affect the quality of the photographs produced. Furthermore, displaying positivity and professionalism at castings will impress clients and improve your chances of securing work. In summary, a good all-round attitude will lead to success, help you to meet the demands of the job and allow you to enjoy the financial and emotional rewards of modelling for years to come.

A strong catwalk technique is essential for a model.

FASHION SHOWS AND HOW TO CATWALK

Your attitude and what it says about you as a model is never more apparent than when you step out on the runway during a fashion show. Whilst your look is important, in order to appear magnificent on the catwalk, you need to consider your walk, knowing how and where to stop, and the way your performance relates to the atmosphere and music. Also, learning how to change outfits quickly backstage will give you the time to prepare for each entrance safe in the knowledge that you look as good as you feel. Equally important as your performance during the show is your behaviour offstage, because with so many models to deal with, as well as the tight

time constraints involved, show producers will rarely tolerate bad behaviour or a lack of professionalism.

Most show days follow a similar pattern, beginning with a call time, clothing fitting, rehearsals, final preparations and then the show itself. Throughout the day, it is each model's responsibility to learn the show choreography, ensure they can make the outfit changes in the given time, know their basic cues and to have seen the hair and make-up department. However, before a model can set foot on a runway, they need to be booked for a fashion show in the first place. This means attending castings where their look and walk are given a very short space of time to impress. Some models complain that they rarely get booked for fashion shows, but fail to consider that their walk might be holding them back.

Just like in photography, a model's eyes should complement the story that the clothes and lighting are trying to tell.

YOUR WALK

Walking is something people do every day and as a working model you'll find yourself doing it more than most. Pounding pavement and going from casting to casting will soon become a way of life, but the most high-profile steps you take will undoubtedly be on the catwalk. Fashion shows are a huge part of the industry and, just like photo shoots, they vary in size, type and location. However, regardless of whether you're modelling on the high fashion runways of Paris and Milan or in a shopping mall in the middle of nowhere, the principles of a good walk, for both boys and girls, are the same.

In principle, a good walk must be confident but not arrogant, focused but not wooden and fluid but not lazy.

Picturing an imaginary tightrope down the centre of the runway can help to begin with, but over time your walk will come more naturally.

Adapt your walk for various outfits. For example, a hand on the hips can accentuate long, flowing gowns by adding extra femininity.

If this seems a lot to think about, then try not to think at all and just walk. A natural walk will be much more likely to impress than an over-the-top, stereotypical walk. Find examples of how high-profile models use the runway and one of the first things you'll notice is the effortlessness and unforced nature of the walk. Take your time and don't rush because being on the runway at even the

I know a model who …

always leers at the girls getting changed backstage. It's so creepy.

At the end of the runway, make a bold statement with a memorable stance. Add individual touches and let your personality shine through.

Your Shoulders, Arms and Hands

Your shoulders should be square and move gently with the flow of your body. A good posture is essential and if you are either too hunched, arched or lopsided, you may find difficulty in perfecting a natural, flowing walk. Various core and postural exercises can help rectify any muscular imbalances (see page 45).

Like your shoulders, your arms should move in unison with your body. There is no need to actively swing them or exaggerate their movement, just let them hang by your side and flow as you move. Your hands and fingers should be completely relaxed, although girls often place one or both hands on their hips to accentuate a feminine walk. If this feels natural, then try it, although it might

Use the full length of the catwalk, but be sure to stay well lit and in full view of the cameras and audience.

smallest fashion show is a really enjoyable experience. Just relax and soak up the atmosphere.

Your Head and Face

Your head should face forward and remain relatively still, and your expression should be one of quiet confidence, although the show producers will direct you about the feel of the show. Sometimes you will be asked to smile, interact with the audience or add personal touches. If you are given little or no direction, then take your inspiration from the clothing, music and general atmosphere and always allow your eyes to show that there is a personality beneath your polished exterior.

be best to let the hand fall by your side at some point during the walk.

Your Feet

Where and how you place your feet will ultimately define your walk. Girls should imagine a straight line down the runway and place one foot in front of the other along this line and from heel to toe. This tightrope-walking method will allow the hips to shift from one side to the other, resulting in a distinctive and feminine walk. Therefore, under no circumstances should boys walk this way. A masculine walk is just an extension of an everyday stroll with added self-assuredness, strength and a hint of non-threatening sex appeal.

How to Stop

Reaching the end of the runway is where even a good walk can come unstuck. Give yourself plenty of time to come to a natural stop by not walking too quickly. As you stop, settle into a natural stance and consider what your face and body are offering to the audience. Just like taking a good photograph, don't pose because posing originates from a very forced and unnatural state of mind. Be mindful of your outfit and showcase its high-lights as best you can.

Where to Stop

Where on the runway to stop is just as important as how to stop. As well as the end of the runway, you may be directed to stop as you enter, exit and at various other points along the way. When approaching the end of the catwalk, don't stop too close to the edge as you might lose the full benefit of the stage lighting. Similarly, stop-ping too soon reduces your time on stage. If you are unsure of where exactly to stop, then double-check with the show producer. They would rather answer questions during rehearsals than work with a silent model who gets it wrong on the night.

The Music

The music will often set the tone for the show and may dictate the speed of your walk. Whilst it's not always advisable to walk on the beat, there are ways to coincide your movement with the music so that the audio complements the visual. Learning an 'eight count' is the easiest way to do this and attending dance classes is recommended for all models. Also, during rehearsals, listen to the phrases within each scene's music track and react accordingly. A well-timed walk in unison with the music is guaranteed to look good.

CHANGING OUTFITS BACKSTAGE

Getting changed quickly is a skill that catwalk models have to learn if they are to meet their cues. Thankfully, you will not be expected to make this change without any assistance and each model is assigned a dresser to help them get out of one outfit and into the next. Sometimes you may share your dresser with another model, but the show producers will always ensure there is someone to organize your next outfit, help you change, and assist you with laces, bows, corsets or other tricky items.

Early in the day, establish a rapport with your dresser, communicate how you like to change and remember to always show them respect. Many dressers have been in the business for years, have worked with countless models and often have the ear of the show producers.

Before you return to the stage, use a mirror to check your appearance. Ensure that nothing is out of place or that any wardrobe malfunctions are unlikely to occur on stage. If for some reason you are likely to miss your cue, then speak up immediately allowing those in charge to help you or adjust the running order accordingly. For example, if a key item of clothing tears during an outfit

Backstage at a fashion show can be a frantic place. It is crucial you stay focused, courteous and professional.

change, it may be decided not to showcase the outfit at all. Alternatively, if it can be quickly disguised, then the audience will never know.

In summary, once you have a walk that secures you work with fashion show producers, you need to perform consistently in order to be considered again for future jobs. You can significantly improve your chances of this happening by taking direction and acting professionally. For example, when given instructions about entry and exit points, as well as basic choreography or walking patterns during rehearsals, pay attention, always stay focused and write down the information to avoid confusion. If you have any questions, they will be answered happily. Leave your mobile phone in your bag!

Just as important as hitting your marks and timing your movements is your personality and performance on stage. If directed to do so, don't be afraid to interact with the audience or other models on the catwalk. Only have a pre-show drink if you are sure that it won't affect your performance and always show the client that you're just as keen for the show to go well as they are.

Lastly, whilst preparations help avoid mistakes, something can still go wrong with the clothing, lighting or music. In fact, the unpredictability of fashion shows are part of what makes the whole experience so exciting. Be adaptable, never hesitate or break character and always show conviction and confidence.

> *A designer is only as good as the star who wears her clothes.*
>
> Edith Head

CASTING TYPES

Castings are one of the most important parts of a model's career. Before you can enjoy all the benefits of working as a model, it is crucial to understand the techniques needed to book consistent and well-paid jobs. A casting is essentially a job interview and, like any other interview, from the moment you walk into the room to meet a potential client, your aim is to convince them that you are the best candidate for the job. A successful model will understand that a honed look and great photos are useless if their casting technique is not right.

There are several types of casting and by understanding the unique challenges they present, you will be better prepared to succeed.

'GO-SEE' CASTING

A 'go-see' usually involves visiting photographers or advertising agencies who do not necessarily have any immediate projects but wish to keep up to date with the pool of models operating within that market. You are most likely to do a go-see when you are a new face, when fresh in a new market or after changing agencies. Go-sees can be a little frustrating because they are usually unlikely to result in immediate work, and without that instant feedback, it can be hard to stay positive about the use of your time. However, it is a great place to make a good first impression as well as a chance to practise your casting technique in a very relaxed and low-pressure environment.

Often, you will be given several go-sees in one day, making it difficult to reach all the appointments on time,

Top Tips for the Catwalk!

- Don't overdo it. A natural walk is far more appealing than a pastiche of a supermodel's walk.

- When changing, the next outfit is always your priority.

- During rehearsals write down all your choreography for each scene. Just before the show starts, refresh yourself with the running order, music and clothing to avoid mistakes.

- If something goes wrong, carry on with confidence. The audience probably won't even notice.

- Bring personality to every walk, even during rehearsals. The show producers and clients might be watching, so always give a good account of yourself.

- Leave your mobile alone and stay focused during the day. If you make a mistake on stage, then you're the one who will look silly.

- Respect your dresser and remember that 'Please' and 'Thank you' take a second to say, but the effects last a lifetime.

but through planning and communication you can save valuable time and energy. Furthermore, by setting off early for the first appointment you'll be able fit a lot more in. Start late and it'll be very difficult to make up the time as the day goes on. If there are unforeseen problems and an appointment time is looking unlikely, then contact your agent to let them know. They can then inform the client and reschedule your appointment. Lateness is inconsiderate and unprofessional, but sometimes unavoidable. Having the courtesy to let the client know will always work in your favour. On arrival, relax and take a minute before the casting to compose yourself and cool down. As stressful as cramming in appointments can be, it's best to avoid taking this baggage into the casting. A bathroom break and a glass of water can work wonders.

While clothes may not make the woman, they certainly have a strong effect on her self-confidence – which, I believe, does make the woman.

Mary Kay Ash

GENERAL/OPEN CASTING

A general casting or 'cattle call' is a way for a client to see all the available models in town and tends to be very busy. Expect long waiting times, but remember that a casting queue is not a supermarket queue and waiting in line with a group of young, good-looking, outgoing boys and girls is a great place to be. Find the positive energy in the room and take that into the casting with you. Laugh, flirt and banter with your fellow models; they are not your competition.

I have made some of the best friends that I've got in this business.

Kate Moss

General castings frequently run for an entire day, sometimes more, which leaves just a few moments for each model with the client. This can be deflating, so maximize your time in front of the client by choosing the right time of day to arrive. Quite frequently clients will be unaware of the number of models waiting to be seen. Although they begin the day with enthusiasm and intend to give everyone equal attention, those arriving late in the day are more likely to be affected by time constraints. In addition, the people present in the casting, like all of us, are human beings who are subject to the effects of fatigue, boredom and hunger. Therefore, if a casting is running between 10am and 5pm, by arriving at 4.55pm, a model can expect to find a tired and hungry client who has seen so many models they couldn't tell the difference between David Gandy and Mahatma Gandhi. Similarly, by arriving too early, the client may still be unsure of the most efficient way to proceed, resulting in the first few arrivals being treated like casting guinea pigs. Choosing to arrive around 10.30am will allow you to present yourself to the client when they are happy and relaxed and quietly enjoying the buzz of their morning coffee. You will be instantly associated with this feeling and later, when the clients review the day's model cards, you will be seen in a much more positive light.

The client is usually holding a general casting because they do not have an exact idea who they are looking for. It can be easy to get lost in the crowd, so be passionate, engaging and vivacious, whilst displaying an air of control and professionalism. By being memorable, you can influence the direction of the production in your favour and because general castings are often for large productions, getting these jobs can be very worthwhile indeed.

AGENCY REQUEST

An agency request is where a client will give an agent an outline of the type of model they are looking for. For example, a brief for a swimwear shoot might be: boys, 20–25, surfer type, blonde hair, 102cm (40in) chest, 81cm (32in) waist. This type of casting is for clients who have a more developed idea who they wish to use but still haven't finalized their decision. Sometimes this brief can be very vague, resulting in these castings being just as busy as general castings but with less time available. They can also be disorganized as the client fails to anticipate the number of models planning to attend. If you arrive and there is no discernible list for the order of entry, take charge of the situation and create one. The other models present, possibly even the client, will see you as a forward-thinking and confident person.

REAL REQUEST

Once a production has a clear vision, the client will browse various agency websites or contact agencies directly and request to see a selection of composite cards. Those models invited to attend are given a specific time slot. Members of the production team, such as the photographer, stylist and advertising executives, are likely to be present, making the casting room a very crowded place. It can be daunting walking into a room with so many pairs of eyes ready to scrutinize your physical appearance, but it is a great opportunity for you to bring your composite card to life. Introduce yourself to each of the clients individually and set a positive tone for the casting. Also, greeting each person individually will give you a chance to relax and settle into a rhythm whilst allowing the client to view first-hand that you are not phased by novel or unfamiliar surroundings. At the very least, you can guarantee they won't forget your name.

SHOW CASTINGS

At fashion show castings models will almost always be asked to walk for the client. This can be in groups or individually. These castings are busy and fast-moving, giving you the least time interacting with the client of any casting type. Speak to the client with your body language by presenting a confident walk. Always remember to take your time, not rush and use every second available. Being silently self-assured can be worth a thousand words, allowing the client to view first-hand that you are capable of strutting your stuff down any runway.

Problem: Your agent will occasionally send you to a casting that, on arrival, you appear not to be right for.

Solution: Trust your agent. They are not in the business of wasting either your or the client's time. If they send you to a casting, it is because they believe you can book the job. If there has been a mistake, then use the opportunity. It is never too late to change the client's mind.

One of the main challenges of show castings is to book the job without the use of your portfolio. Not being able to rely on one of your main tools increases the need for you to impress the client with just your look and attitude. However, if you are new to the business then your book might not necessarily be your strongest asset anyway. Show castings give you the chance to display your full potential without the need to worry about the length or strength of your portfolio.

TELEVISION COMMERCIAL CASTINGS

A television commercial (TVC) casting will almost always be hosted by a casting director with a video camera at one end of the room and a plain background at the other. The client is sometimes present, but if they are not, then their intention is to review the videotaped performances at a later date. Given that this will be your only contact with the client, it is important to speak to your booker prior to the casting and research the retailer online. You'll find that by paying attention to the brand's demographic, you can begin to sculpt your appearance closer to the client's vision. For example, a boy can look very different with a shave, a shirt and a tie and similarly for girls, a simple change of outfit, make-up and hairstyle can drastically alter the image you portray.

On arrival, you will be asked to fill out a form with your personal details, measurements and previous commercial work. Once completed, the casting assistant will take a polaroid and then you will be given a few minutes to familiarize yourself with the script or storyboard before being invited into the studio. Learning this in a short amount of time can be daunting and trying to remember the lines along with direction adds to the pressure, so be sure to arrive early. This added time will give you more of a chance to familiarize yourself with the material, allowing your focus to rest on the emotion behind the words. Take the script elsewhere and perform it aloud considering movement, actions and how you aim to bring your personality to the role. Alternatively, ask your agent if they can send you the script or storyboard beforehand as you will have more time to prepare and in the privacy of your own home. You are more likely to deliver a better performance if you are not wholly dependent on the script during recording.

Once invited into the studio, and after the introductions, the casting director will ask for an Ident to camera, which involves you giving your name, agent's details and maybe offering a little information about yourself. Use the Ident to your advantage by showing yourself to be relaxed and at ease in front of the camera. Talk about your hobbies, interests or studies and give examples of situations that challenge your mind and body. This will not only let the client see there is more to you than modelling but will also relax you, giving you time to adjust to the surroundings. You will also be asked to show your profiles and your hands so the client has a better understanding of how you look and move from various angles.

Once the Ident is completed, the casting director will speak to you about the script and offer some direction for your performance. Never be afraid to ask questions and make sure you understand exactly what is required of you. The casting director will be focused on helping you as much as possible. Furthermore, when they do give you hints and pointers, absorb this information and incorporate it into your performance. Soon after, the camera will roll and your performance will be captured.

One of the challenges of casting for a TVC is how easily a model can become self-aware or feel a bit silly. Relax; the casting director has seen it all before. You will not be the best actor they have ever worked with and you certainly won't be the worst. Indeed, trying to 'act' out a scene will result in a performance that appears awkward and disingenuous. The script is not designed to catch you out and like any conversation it will have a flow. Try actually listening to your cue lines and react in an honest and natural way. Also, more important than the words on the paper are your levels of self-assurance and the way you respond to the situation.

Often, you will be asked to record the same scene in different ways and, occasionally, you are asked to develop the role in a way you might not normally choose, but it is essential to follow the direction closely, adapt quickly and be as versatile as possible. If in doubt, step it up a notch; from a casting director's point of view, it's easier to calm a performance down than to push for more.

Take your time because by not rushing through your casting, you'll allow yourself enough time to settle into the role. Finally, it may sound obvious but always wait until the casting director has cued you for action and don't break character until you are told to do so.

Recalls

If all goes well at your initial TVC casting, then you may be asked back for a recall. The client will be present as well as the director of the television commercial and other members of the team. You may be given a revised version of the script, other actors to work with or simply asked to repeat your original performance. If you've been asked back, then don't change too much unless instructed to do so.

FITTINGS/SHOWROOM CASTINGS

Casting for fittings or showroom will typically involve having measurements taken and being asked to try on a few garments. It's all about how the clothing fits, which means if a model is the wrong size, they are unlikely to book the job. If a model is requested to attend, it is because the client's criteria and the model's measurements are similar, if not an exact match. However, if the measurements provided on the model's composite card are inaccurate, it wastes both the model's and the client's time. Be honest on your card and if your measurements change, then let your agent know. Also, immediately before the casting try not to eat a big meal or pump any iron as these small changes in your body shape can make all the difference.

As with any casting, your attitude plays a massive part in whether you book the job or not. Every model at the casting might fit the clothes, but small touches like folding or hanging garments will show you to be a responsible and respectful person. Personal hygiene is particularly important because getting measured can be a very up-close experience.

Ultimately, securing a good showroom/fitting client who will book you consistently throughout the year, regardless of the season or trend, is a valuable asset. Minute differences in body shapes are not nearly as important as your manner.

MODEL AGENCY CASTINGS

Bookers from around the world will often travel to other markets and hold castings for models they might like to represent. Agents and bookers are very experienced at selecting who they need for their agency's books, making it hard to convince them otherwise. On the plus side, they are rarely blinkered and are often quick to spot potential. Even if they currently have other models similar to you or are on the hunt for this season's look, by making a good impression you can set a foundation for travelling to other markets and expanding your career. The fastest way to impress an overseas booker is to show an interest in travelling to their proposed market. Research the city that you are hoping visit, taking note of the type of model who usually works there as well as the established client base.

CRASHING CASTINGS

Attending uninvited or 'crashing' a casting is always a contentious issue and has raised much debate within the industry. Some view casting-crashing as professionally discourteous to fellow models and few appreciate an unwanted guest eating into their valuable casting time. From the client's point of view this can also be viewed as extremely rude and undermines the casting's validity. After all, if a model is sent to a casting as part of an agency or real request, it is because the client has spent time and energy narrowing their brief to a point where those who aren't invited are probably not right for the job. Subsequently, a model who crashes a casting could result in their booker being reprimanded, causing trouble for the agency. This, in turn, could jeopardize the crasher's career, as they may be excluded from future productions involving a particular casting director.

However, this behaviour can be perceived as gutsy, confident and with just the right amount of cheek. A casting director may even respect your determination and initiative. Occasionally for casting crashers, the outcome can be positive, resulting in a recall, or at best booking the job.

If you notice a casting taking place that you're not invited to and the models requested are of a similar look and age group to yourself, then your first course of action should be to contact your agent. Find out what the casting is for and whether the agency was aware of its existence. Your agent will either give you the green light to attend, or at the very least you will have an explanation as to why you weren't invited. If you decide to crash a casting anyway, it is vital to ask permission and

be honest. It's not recommended, but as always, the decision is yours.

QUEUE-JUMPING

Unlike crashing a casting, there is no real upside to jumping a queue. It is rude and shows disrespect to your fellow models. From time to time a model will have a genuine excuse for not waiting, but if you plan your daily schedule correctly, there should be little reason ever to resort to this.

In conclusion, there are many different types of casting, all with their own unique set of challenges. However, turning each novel situation to your advantage can make castings an enjoyable and fruitful part of your day.

CASTING TECHNIQUES

There are many different variations of castings, but all are basically job interviews and therefore, regardless of the type of casting you are attending, there are some universal techniques you can employ before, during and after that will significantly improve your chances of booking that job.

BEFORE

Prepare for the casting by researching the client and their product. The Internet offers a wealth of information on just about anyone or anything. Explore your potential client's demographic, sales history or even share price. This will give you an idea of how to dress, your hairstyle and possible topics of discussion. This also works when casting for bookers from foreign markets. Research the agency's website, looking for any models who may be in your age range or who have a similar look to you. Also, research the cities themselves and ask yourself whether they are places you would like to visit, work in or even live in.

Believe in Yourself

Finding confidence can sometimes be a tricky task, but if you don't believe in yourself, then neither will the client. Always remember that you have just as much right to be at the casting as anyone else. If your agent believes in you enough to send you to see the client and invest their time and energy in you, then the least you can do is believe in yourself.

I'm competitive with myself. I always try to push past my own borders.

Tyra Banks

Don't Rush

Never be in a rush to see the client. If you don't feel 100 per cent ready, then let the next model on the list go before you. Those few extra minutes can be used to compose yourself, cool down and get in the right frame of mind, making it easier to present a calm and confident persona.

DURING

During a casting, your main aim is to uncover the needs of the potential client and present yourself as the ideal candidate to meet those needs. This is impossible unless you talk to the client and the fastest way to establish this rapport is with the three 'E's of castings: to engage, enthuse and empathize.

Engage

Once you have introduced yourself, your first priority is to engage the client in a conversation about the upcoming project. By doing this, they will immediately associate you with the project even if you are not their ideal candidate. Ask questions about the project, even if you know the answers from previous conversations with your agent or as a result of your diligent brand research online.

Enthuse

Once a conversation is underway, appear enthusiastic about the idea being proposed. Advertisers are likely to have spent a lot of time and energy in development by

Possible questions to ask include:

- What is the theme/feel of the shoot?
- Who is the photographer?
- Where are you shooting?
- Whose idea was the project?

the time they are ready to cast a model. By showing interest in their ideas, they will feel confident that you are excited to work with them and, if booked, would be a valid member of the production.

Empathize

No production is without its problems. Locations, weather and overbearing bosses can all have an effect on the development of a project. By offering the client your empathy and reassuring them that it will be a worthwhile venture, you can present yourself as a professional who understands the needs of the client as well as the demands of the task ahead.

One very important point to remember is that no casting is a waste of time and even if you are not chosen

If you have any particularly interesting or extreme hobbies, bring them up at castings and show there is more to you than meets the eye.

for that particular job, a positive impression can last as long as your career and beyond. Above all else, the client needs to know that you do not fit any of the stereotypes that are still present in the fashion industry. Models can be viewed as either lazy, vain, self-centred or all of the above. But, by following the three 'E's, you can engage a client in a five-minute conversation, and appear hard-working and likeable without the need to mention yourself once.

Create a Positive Atmosphere in the Room

Modelling is a fun, exciting and lucrative job, so celebrate that fact in a casting. The client will see you as a positive and energetic person; in other words, the type of person they might like to work with. Shoot days can be stressful for the client, but for the most part a photo shoot represents the culmination of months of hard word and a realization of their vision. It should be a fun, vibrant and positive place, so if a model shows up to the casting whining about public transport, the weather or the length of the casting queue, they are immediately stating that if the shoot is not going according to plan they are likely to add to the problem. Instead, find the silver lining in a situation and be seen as a solution not a problem.

Use Eye Contact to Control the Casting

Eye contact is crucial for any social interaction and castings are no exception. Entire books have been written on the importance of eye contact and since modelling owes so much to the eyes and the emotions conveyed within them, it is very important to strike a nice balance when meeting potential clients for the first time. Too much eye contact and a model can appear overly intense or desperate. Equally, too little can given an impression of timidness, aloofness or even arrogance. Neither of these contribute to a positive outcome and so the best course is to offer a little eye contact and then divert the client's attention with a gentle glance towards your portfolio. Once they take the cue, then you are free to either offer eye contact to another member of the casting team or completely change the direction of the conversation to the photographs before them.

At the beginning of a casting it is important to offer equal attention to all present, but throughout its course it usually becomes apparent who the decision-maker is.

Without excluding the others, subtly divert your attention in their direction by offering them the greatest share of your eye contact. However, fashion is not fascism, so ignore the other members of the team at your peril. Whilst the decision-makers have the final say, having as many people on your side as possible can be the difference between an option or confirmation.

If done well, you can control the pace and direction on a casting with just a few minuscule movements of your eye.

Play Hard to Get

By appearing busy, even if you are not, you can project the image of a model who is in demand, and once the client knows you are a successful model, they will view you accordingly. It is also useful to pause in thought before answering questions about your availability. This pause is a way of subtly conveying that whilst you are busy, you are also prepared to fit them into your schedule. Both the above are very powerful statements to make, but there are a few dangers in giving a false illusion. Firstly, don't lie to the client by creating photo shoots or shows, or even saying you got jobs that you didn't. For example, the photographer's assistant might have worked on a job that you are claiming as your own and expose you as a liar either during or after the casting. Similarly, if you are at a casting for Coca Cola, don't commit yourself to a fictional Pepsi shoot.

AFTER

If a casting is unsuccessful, it can sometimes help to ask your agent for any available feedback from the client. Modelling can sometimes be a strange combination of acceptance and rejection and by understanding the reasons behind the client's decision, you can put your mind at rest. Also, by letting your agent know that you are willing to constantly try to improve as a model, they will view you in higher esteem, thereby strengthening your relationship. Most importantly, you can further improve your performance by repeating the areas that worked and phasing out those that didn't. If, for example, the client felt that your book was not strong enough, then do a test.

You may still receive positive feedback even if you didn't book the job. If the production went in a different

Top Tips for Castings!

- Plan to arrive early and if all goes according to plan, you can use this extra time to relax and prepare.

- Always make an impression as long as it's a good one.

- When discussing the photography in your portfolio, speak about elements such as the light, photographer, styling and crew. It doesn't always have to be about you.

- There is no such thing as a wasted casting and good networking will always pay off in the end.

- Leave life's problems at the door and always present an easy manner and sunny disposition.

- Actually listen to what is being asked of you and react accordingly.

direction but they liked your look, energy and enthusiasm, the client might add that they hope to work with you at a future date.

YOU AND YOUR AGENT

The role of an agent is so much more than just a person who passively acts as a bridge between clients and models. Your booker is a hard-working salesperson who aims to promote you to almost everyone they speak to. As well as finding castings, liaising with clients, negotiating rates, chasing buyouts, organizing your book, generating your cards, updating your website, chasing photography, placing you abroad and seeking out new opportunities, they also act as day-to-day problem-solvers who strive to ensure that all situations end in your favour. Most importantly, they are the first person you should go to for advice and counsel about your career. After all, your agency decided to represent you because they saw your potential and personality and had a vision for your future.

It could be argued that all of the above are simply parts of a booker's job description and if a model doesn't work, the agency doesn't collect its percentage or booking fee, but as a bond grows, it is clear that your

booker will become more than just a business associate and can act as a personal confidante and friend. Whilst is important for the boundaries between business and friendship to not blur, it is vital to understand that the strength of this relationship depends on trust, communication and respect.

You trust that your agent will promote you in the most favourable way possible to the right clients and recover any money you're owed in due course. In addition, you trust that they have your best interests at heart and are as concerned with your long-term goals as your potential to generate short-term revenue. Equally, your agent trusts that you will repay their faith by using your look, your book and your attitude to convert castings and other opportunities into paid work. Furthermore, once booked for work, they trust that you have the organizational skills and professionalism to carry out the task in a way that reflects favourably on you and the agency as a whole. Ultimately, if all the models at an agency exhibit these qualities, the brand as a whole achieves a reputation to be envied.

The fastest way to build trust is with honest and constant communication. One reason why this is so important is because of the ratio of models to bookers at an agency. Busy bookers at large agencies can be responsible for anywhere between 50 to 100 models. With such little time to spend on each individual, it can be easy for models to feel either neglected or unwanted. However, with the right amount of communication, you'll always feel good about your place and be able to discuss matters in an honest and open way. As well as talking to your bookers during the daily check-in, a good booker will always be contactable throughout the working day. A phone call is usually enough to answer any questions or niggling concerns, although it is best not to call during their lunch hour as everyone deserves a break. Similarly, you should always be available by phone, email or text and between the hours of 9am and 6pm, personal matters take second place. The speed at which booking decisions are made mean that if a model is unreachable for even a few hours, the work might get passed on to the next available person. If you do miss a call, then it is essential to return messages as soon as possible, and when receiving emails or texts, to respond with a simple confirmation. This acts as a professional courtesy, as well as ensuring that your agent has no doubt that you have received the message.

Communication is never more important than when things aren't going as planned. For example, a model unable to secure steady or good-quality work because of a quiet market, a card that isn't working or something else they hadn't considered, will need a speedy solution to kick-start their career. However, rather than suffering in silence, complaining to other models or even thinking of changing agency, they should, instead, speak to their bookers. As well as offering reassurances, bookers may suggest testing or travelling to foreign markets to book-build. They may also arrange fresh go-see appointments with fitting and showroom clients to ensure a reliable revenue stream. Whichever solution is presented, you can guarantee that the strategies to generate work will be accompanied by an agent who is aware of the problem and who will redouble their efforts. After all, a happy model has a happy booker and vice versa. If you find yourself in this situation, make an appointment to sit down and discuss the problem with your booker and never try to resolve more serious issues with an email. Intentions can be confused because written messages offer neither a chance for immediate response or the benefit of voice tone, eye contact and body language. For that matter, neither is a phone call the best way to problem-solve. By talking face-to-face with your booker, you can guarantee their undivided attention, solve the problem faster and gain their respect.

One way to avoid this worst-case scenario of long spells without work is to have regular chats about your career and implement any advice given. In short, you should take the initiative and develop as a model. The role an agent plays in your development is very much a personal decision and it begins the day you sign your contract. Every model is given access to agency contacts, expertise and any other tools at their disposal, but you will only improve your earning potential by taking those opportunities. For example, if your agent recommends a photographer and passes on their details, then it is your responsibility to contact the photographer, arrange the shoot and retrieve the contact sheets, from which your booker can select the final pictures.

One area of development that is perhaps less obvious is coming to terms with the balance of power in the model/booker relationship. The way this shifts over a career can determine your long-term success, and the faster an equilibrium is found, the happier both parties will be. Firstly, this shouldn't be a parent/child relationship, whereby a booker needs to constantly spoonfeed information, tests and work to a model. Furthermore, they shouldn't have to constantly chase unreliable or irresponsible models or make excuses to clients for unprofessional behaviour. This quickly becomes tiresome and unless a model learns to stand on their own two feet, interest soon fades, regardless of how good a model's look is.

Equally, a model should not believe that their success lies entirely in the hands of their agency. As new faces, most models are heavily dependent on the advice and support of their bookers. Then, if things aren't working out, they become resentful and feel either undervalued, mistreated or condescended to. Also, they may think that other agencies carry more prestige and are able to open doors to a potentially better and larger base of clients. As a result of this discontent, they switch agencies and, once again, become heavily dependent on the advice and support of their new bookers, believing that their success lies entirely in the hands of their agency. At first, the change feels justified by an initial surge in castings and business, only to find that they eventually fall back into the same patterns and are treated in a similar way as before. This is because they fail to develop, repeat the same mistakes and never quite realize that the relationship doesn't have to be equal, as long as it is equitable. Just remember that your career satisfaction depends on the time and effort you put into your work, and it is this that will bring you rewards.

The relationship will find a nice balance and, whilst it is true that some agencies are bigger, more efficiently run, offer unique possibilities or have a higher class of model on their books, there is rarely a fast track to fortune. Most clients realize that the industry has

I know a model who …

is always speaking negatively about their agent. One day the agent heard about this and told them to seek alternative representation.

changed and that all agencies can offer capable models. There are occasions when a change of agent is for the best and no one should make you feel bad, question your ability or damage your self-esteem. Above all else, remember that you control your career and your decisions are final. Your agent is there to advise you as best they can and is neither your parent, your boss or your employee.

Also, although the majority of your dealings are with your own bookers, you should be friendly towards all the bookers at your agency. Smaller tasks like checking-in or minor queries can be made easier if you are liked and respected by all the staff.

Finally, whilst this relationship should be as efficient and professional as possible, you should never lose a sense of fun and light-hearted banter.

BREAKING THE STEREOTYPE

We've all heard about the model stereotype: self-obsessed, hedonistic and just a little bit vacant. Whilst it would be convenient to say that this stereotype exists only through jealousy, misunderstanding or because high-profile scandals make great tabloid headlines, the truth is that there are models who still display these qualities. Furthermore, this stereotype exists within the industry itself. Quite often, advertisers, show producers, casting agents, photographers and even bookers will view all models negatively unless given good reason to think otherwise.

By recognizing and side-stepping these labels, you can avoid being pigeonholed as 'just another model'. Better still, by breaking the stereotype and showing yourself to be much more, you can pleasantly surprise clients as well as disarm any prospective doubters.

Stereotype: Models don't eat
Solution: The lunch bunch

Lunchtime is always a nice chance to sit down with the crew and discuss anything and everything except work, but it can also be difficult to stick to your healthy eating plan. Quite often studios have in-house chefs, whilst on location it is more likely that food will be delivered or bought from a nearby supermarket. Either way, food can vary in quality, nutritional value and amount depending on the location, production budget and the tastes of the team. However, one thing is consistent: clients and crew will certainly notice a model who complains about the food, so unless you have special dietary requirements or allergies, then always eat what's on offer and be sure to show your gratitude. This doesn't mean a model should feast or overindulge; just let the client know that you have a healthy attitude towards food and that you are not obsessed by calorie counts. Furthermore, later in the day your energy level will not suffer and neither will your work. If you are a fussy eater, particularly strict about your diet or have allergies, then it is your responsibility to prepare for this in advance by bringing a packed lunch.

- Don't chance it. Bring your own food, energy shakes or at least some healthy snacks.
- Eat and keep your energy up; it might be a long day.
- Photo studios are filled with chocolate, crisps and biscuits. Resist!

Stereotype: Models are self-absorbed
Solution: The name game

One of the fastest ways to get into people's good books is to remember their name. This shows that you are a good listener and not solely concerned with the sound of your own voice. However, on a shoot day, for example, it is not uncommon to meet up to ten new people and recalling all of their names can prove tricky. Therefore, whenever you're booked for a job, ask your agent in advance for a copy of the call sheet. If you can't get your hands on a call sheet, then one technique to remember a person's name is to use it a couple of times during the introduction.

This technique should usually be enough, but if you do forget, then do not hesitate to politely ask again.

- Get a call sheet from your agent.
- Listen during introductions rather than waiting for your turn to speak.
- Don't be afraid to ask again.
- Don't overuse a person's name. It can seem disingenuous.

'I call this look "Blue steel"...' Avoid the Hollywood clichés about models with a good attitude and realistic outlook.

However, after a certain amount of time it can prove socially awkward to admit to forgetting a person's name, so listen out for others using it, refer to your call sheet or quietly ask one of the other models.

Stereotype: Models are lazy
Solution: Assist the assistants

Photographers' assistants, runners and studio hands can easily be overlooked at photo shoots or whilst filming commercials. However, the days would be a lot harder, longer and less enjoyable without their tireless work, so where you can, help them out, engage with them and at the very least always be polite. Small things like helping to carry a bag when on location or offering someone a coffee can make a massive difference that people may remember for years.

Stereotype: Models are stupid
Solution: It's not rocket science

You don't have to discuss quantum mechanics to let people know you have a brain. Fashion is a very social industry and if you engage people on any level, it will show that there is more to you than just the obvious. If you can't think of a subject, then chat about something

you're passionate about: your interests, hobbies, likes and dislikes – anything as long as it's not modelling. However, be careful not talk about yourself too much (remember the stereotype about models being self-absorbed?).

- Be social and fun. A sense of humour is a sign of intelligence.
- Don't talk too much and if you can't think of anything to say, then just listen.

In summary, models who exhibit stereotypical behaviour simply remind people of the industry's negative side. Instead, surprise the team and overturn their preconceptions. They'll see you as down-to-earth and easy to work with. If you are ever stuck for inspiration on how to remain humble, respectful and positive, bear in mind how privileged you are to be able to do this job. Always make the most of it and remember there is a massive difference between 'being' a model and 'working' as one. By thinking of modelling as a vocation rather than allowing yourself to be defined by it, you'll be able to maintain a level head and ultimately enjoy the benefits of the job for a lot longer.

DEALING WITH THE DEMANDS OF THE JOB

Although modelling can be viewed as a carefree and easy existence, anyone who has modelled for a significant period will tell you that at times it certainly isn't as glamorous as people think. Learning to not only deal with the demands of the job but also to turn them to your advantage is the secret to long-lasting success and happiness. Level of Commitment: You Get Out What You Put In

Modelling is not a 9 to 5 job, which means you can't always leave work at the office. Therefore, determination and a degree of self-discipline are a must, because the amount of time and energy you are prepared to invest will undoubtedly affect your level of success. This may mean going to the gym on a Sunday morning when you would rather watch TV or traipsing across a city to go to a casting in the pouring rain. Remember: whilst every model's career path is different, few make it to the top overnight and although modelling is a unique, enjoyable and lucrative way to earn a living, you still have to earn it. With the benefits come an expectation of results, and in an increasingly busy marketplace there will always be someone else ready to fill your shoes if you are not prepared to work for your success.

REJECTION: DON'T TAKE IT PERSONALLY, IT'S JUST BUSINESS

A robust self-esteem as well as the ability not to take rejection personally are vital qualities to possess. Dealing with daily rejection based on your physical appearance could be considerably disheartening if taken out of context, but by understanding that it is a necessary part of the industry, you can learn to let it pass you by. Of course, constructive criticism should always be listened

I don't think I've ever been a model. I don't think of myself as a model. I love images. I like the composition.

Eva Herzigova

A smart model is a good model.

Tyra Banks

to, but learning not to take it personally allows you to be exposed to the full extent of people's opinions whilst maintaining a healthy outlook.

You won't book every job because each client has a subjective viewpoint about what is best for their vision. Try to maintain a positive mental attitude and remember that one phone call from your agent can change everything.

YOUR PLACE IN SOCIETY: WORK AS A MODEL, DON'T ACT LIKE ONE

The end product of a photo shoot or fashion show is often very glamorous and as a result there are certain myths and misconceptions that surround the industry. Subsequently, preconceived notions about models can follow you around. Try to learn to accept that some people will view you in a certain way because of what you do. Some models like to deal with this by not divulging what they do for a living until they feel comfortable in the company they are keeping. Alternatively, you can go further: allow people their preconceived notions about what it is to work as a model and then surprise them by breaking the stereotype.

I was 14 when I started modelling. At the end of that first day my mum said, 'If you want to do this, you're on your own because I'm not traipsing around London ever again like that. It's a nightmare.'

Kate Moss

I know a model who ...

refuses to wear any shoes but her own. What's more, she actually says this to clients at the casting. No wonder she never gets jobs.

COMPETITION: YOU ARE A BEAUTIFUL AND UNIQUE SNOWFLAKE

Whilst the world of modelling is often seen as a competitive place, it is crucial that you don't compete with the models around you. Each model possesses a unique look, commercial viability and skill set, and by wasting energy worrying about everyone else, a model can lose focus on the real goal of achieving financial success and job satisfaction. If you don't book a job, then this time you weren't what the client was looking for, whether that's because you didn't have the right look, or your book wasn't strong enough or a million other reasons. Either way, dwelling on who did book the job will only bring negativity into your life, and that never helps.

Consider your relationship with other models like that of members of an Olympic athletics squad. Some specialize in track events whilst others excel in the field. Occasionally it might feel like you're running in the same race against your teammates, but in the end, by providing support and working off each other's energy in castings, on shoots or at shows, you'll find the experience infinitely more enjoyable. Clients will also respond to your positivity and easy-going manner.

TRAVEL: THE WORLD IS A SMALL PLACE

Travelling to locations and living around the world can be fun and exciting but also comes at a cost. Living out of a suitcase for weeks at a time can be tiring and expensive roaming charges might dissuade a model from calling home. However, by using webcams, social networking sites, emails and texts, you can stay in contact with your friends and family and there is no reason to feel isolated when abroad.

Work trips often involve shooting for many consecutive hours with early starts, sometimes in extreme weather conditions. Stay positive and make the most of your trips abroad, and remember that whatever the conditions, you are not stuck in behind a desk doing a job you hate.

RESPECT: R.E.S.P.E.C.T.

From the moment you are booked for a job, try and consider yourself as part of the production team and no more important than the other members of the crew. However, respect works both ways and if you feel genuinely uncomfortable or undervalued, then don't be afraid to voice your concerns to either the client, your agent, or both.

In conclusion, whilst there must be elements of security and robustness in your personality to begin with, you can easily develop these qualities. Maturing into a balanced and secure person takes confidence and self-assurance, the ability to pick yourself up after a knock-back and not to take it too personally. Remember: as a model you are dispensable, but this has no bearing on you as a person, and if you meet the daily challenges of the industry head on, you can develop into an excellent model who will be booked again and again.

- Treat everyone with the respect that you would expect in return.
- Photo shoots are a team effort, so make the effort for your team.
- Your job is to model, so don't help at the expense of your own role.

Final Thoughts on . . .
Your Attitude

There are enough models out there who are gorgeous and good looking, but have nothing to bring. They can take good pictures, but after that, when you take the pictures, what do you have to say for yourself?

Coco Rocha

You are not a model if you don't work as one, which makes your daily castings an absolute priority. Converting potential clients into paid work is a challenge that should be relished and not viewed as a chore, so at the very least try to enjoy the experience. You'll find that clients respond to your positivity and grounded outlook and view you as an intriguing prospect for future productions. Once you've secured the work, a good attitude will make you a pleasure to work with, which significantly improves your chances of repeat bookings. Above all else, remember that the demands of the job are a lot easier to meet if you take your work seriously while still having fun with it.

KEEPING IT FRESH

YOUR LOOK

Keeping your look fresh can be as simple as tweaking your hairstyle or as radical as completely overhauling your body shape. There are several factors to consider before you begin to tamper with the image you present to clients. Firstly, ask yourself whether your proposed change will negatively affect your relationship with your existing clients, and also if the new look is likely to appeal to potential new clients. Both are educated guesses and you can never really predict the outcome, but there are indicators, such as the trend for the coming season, the success of other models with a similar look and the guidance of your agent.

YOUR BOOK

Keeping your book fresh is easy if you never consider it to be 'complete'. It can always be updated with tests and recent tears or completely restructured and stripped back depending on markets, seasons and career paths. Equally, a new card once or twice every six to eight months should show clients your ability to adapt as well as your extensive catalogue of great photographs.

YOUR ATTITUDE

Keeping a fresh attitude can be difficult without a sense of progression and as a self-employed model it can be easy to feel professionally static. Furthermore, without a distinction between the office and home, this sense of inertia can creep into all aspects of a model's life. Therefore, the secret to remaining motivated is to always set goals: not only as a model, but also as a person. This will help you easily distinguish between the two strands of your life. For example, professionally you could set a goal to increase your annual income by 10 per cent or to work with a particular photographer. Meanwhile, in your personal life you could aim to learn a new language or take up an instrument. Frequently, a goal can crossover into both aspects of your life. Acting classes or taking up a new sport are activities you may gain great personal satisfaction from and may also benefit your career.

Regardless of the goal, achievements are always coupled by a sense of progression and whilst the length, size and tangibility of these goals can vary greatly, the important aspect of goal-setting is that you feel like you're moving forward.

It is important not to set unrealistic goals or to get too disheartened if you do not meet expectations. Just bear in mind that your level of commitment will directly affect the results and if you really apply yourself, you're likely to have more success than if you don't. A massive perk of modelling is that you have more time than most people at your disposal. How you choose to use it is up to you.

MODELLING IN OTHER MARKETS

Wherever you begin your journey as a model, it is advisable to travel to other countries and break into new markets. Generating new clients across the globe is not only a healthy expansion of your business, but also a great excuse to see new cultures and experience different ways of life. However, deciding where to visit, when to travel, how long to stay, how it might affect your career and the professional challenges involved, should all be considered before booking your ticket and heading off.

The first step is to talk to your agent and discuss how an extended stay in a foreign market might benefit you. There are some markets that are seasonal and even those that are not still have busier periods and specific dates worth noting. For example, each market has its own fashion week, where designers showcase their latest collections in a series of runway shows. Therefore, London, Milan, Paris and New York's fashion weeks are a great opportunity to display your look and attitude on the catwalk. Making a good impression can result in a major campaign booking, but during this time, fashion week dominates the industry and if you are not featuring in the shows, travelling to these markets is a waste of time.

Once you have decided what time of year to visit, it is important to consider at what stage in your career each market will benefit you the most. Some markets are extremely lucrative, but you can expect experienced models with a strong book. Alternatively, some destinations are best visited specifically to work on your portfolio. Either way, your mother agent will know which markets are best suited to you and in which ones they can boost your career.

ATHENS
The Market
Athens is a market that is heavily geared towards swimwear, catalogues and television commercials. Nevertheless, there are still many opportunities for models to shoot tests and editorials and acquire a number of good-quality tear sheets. Magazines are produced very quickly, which means that a model is able to return to their home market after two months with a book displaying a range of styles, locations and photographers. Also, attaining a visa for some countries means providing many examples of work and the volume of work available in Athens can help with this.

The Lifestyle
Athens is ideally to suited to younger models who can take advantage of the vibrant social scene but are happy to share cramped and expensive model apartments. The city can get fiercely hot in the summer, and the unreliable public transport and confusing layout of the city mean that castings are often hard to get to. However, these are all part of the city's charm and Athens is an exciting city with a great energy.

Visa and Work Permit Considerations
Citizens of the European Union (EU) are able to live and work in Greece without a visa or work permit. For non-EU citizens the working holiday visa for visitors aged eighteen to thirty is the best option for most models. This allows foreign national models to work for up to a year, but can only used once.

CAPE TOWN
The Market
Africa's most developed fashion market is in Cape Town, South Africa, due to the city's stunning locations, beautiful light, guaranteed fair weather between November and March and the cheap production costs. During this time, clients from all over the world travel to Cape Town to shoot catalogues, commercials and campaigns and by timing your arrival, you can take advantage of the large amount of work available. The only real downside is that international clients will generally pay a reduced day rate to cover the cost of flying and accommodating their crew. In fact, models often find themselves shooting for regular clients who pre-empt their visit to Cape Town and book them locally to save money. On the plus side,

Athens is a city of great charm and its classical heritage belies its vibrant social scene.

Warm weather and fantastic light make Cape Town a photographer's dream.

impressing international clients can often lead to securing additional work throughout the year.

The Lifestyle

Although the living costs in South Africa are very reasonable, due to the weakness of the rand, most models find it difficult to return home with a significant amount of money, even if they worked constantly. Nonetheless, for the duration of a stay, the warm climate and golden beaches make for a memorable experience and as long as you stay vigilant and protect yourself and your belongings at all times, the high crime rate that blights much of South Africa shouldn't affect you. Take pre-booked taxis when travelling around the city, don't flaunt expensive items and avoid travelling alone if possible.

Visa and Work Permit Considerations

Work permits are easily acquired for South Africa and last up to either one year, which means that you will have to repeat the process if you wish to return season after season, or three to five years for an additional fee.

Alternatively, for a short trip, a letter of invitation from your South African agency, specifying the duration of your stay, will secure you up to three months' valid entry. It must be presented to passport control on arrival.

HAMBURG

The Market

Germany is one of the largest catalogue markets in the world and Hamburg offers models a chance to rapidly expand their client base in a very short amount of time. In just two weeks it is possible to travel around the city and see a long list of catalogues, production companies and advertising agencies. However, expectations of models are high in Germany, so it is better to visit once you have built your book and have a carefully honed look. On the plus side, a positive attitude is really well received and client loyalty is especially high. Often clients will ignore geography and fly you from almost anywhere if they know you're up to the job. It is not really necessary to stay for more than a month, and although there are productions throughout the year, August and December represent a quieter time.

Hamburg – clean, green and with an excellent public transport network.

The Lifestyle

The currency is the euro and the living costs are comparable to most European cities. The standard of life in Hamburg is very good; it is a clean, green place with a very good public transport system and easy bicycle hire. The city has a variety of distractions and the nightlife on the Reeperbahn is a particular highlight. Always take both sunblock and an umbrella as the weather conditions in northern Germany are extremely variable.

Visa and Work Permit Considerations

For EU residents, no visa is required, although the German government can take a fair slice of your earnings, which you cannot claim back unless you are VAT-registered. For non-EU residents the process is relatively simple as long as you are prepared to fill out the extensive forms and provide the correct documentation. Arrive on a standard, three-month Schengen tourist visa and then apply for a residence permit which costs 60 euros.

HONG KONG

The Market

The market in Hong Kong is as varied as anything you'll find in the rest of the world. China's burgeoning economy means that there is plenty of work for both commercial and editorial models alike and the high rates can make a trip there financially rewarding. However, a high standard of look, book and attitude are all expected and it is perhaps better suited to more experienced models. Hong Kong fashion week is always a good time to visit.

The Lifestyle

There are over seven million inhabitants crammed into this tiny city, making it a very busy and intense place to live in. Restaurants, bars, shops and other distractions are always open for business and at all hours of the day and night. The cost of living is moderate, the nightlife is frenetic and the public transport system is first class. Overall, few come away from Hong Kong without having had a positive and memorable experience, although the humidity can make life uncomfortable. Also, air pollution is evermore problematic as neighbouring Chinese provinces continue to become industrialized.

Visa and Work Permit Considerations

Obtaining a visa for work in Hong Kong is relatively straightforward because companies need to prove that the position cannot be filled by a local. Of course, every

Hong Kong: busy, cramped and humid but truly unforgettable.

model's unique look helps them to meet this criteria and as long as your agency in Hong Kong sends a letter of invitation and you fill out the appropriate information at your nearest Chinese embassy, you can have a visa processed relatively quickly. On arrival, one of the first things you'll notice is that all immigration officials speak fluent English, making it possible to deal with any problems easily.

LONDON
The Market
The market in London is so varied and widespread that, except for the last two weeks of the year when the industry shuts down, every variety of model, at any stage of a career, should be able to secure regular and well-paid work. As well as having a very vibrant commercial market, London is also home to fashion houses and well-respected editorial magazines. Therefore, it is a great place to build a portfolio and then cash in. Furthermore, the English pound is one of the strongest currencies in the world, making London even more attractive in budgetary terms. On the downside, production budgets are not always huge, clients prefer to use models who stay for at least three months and the UK is a relatively small usage territory.

The Lifestyle
It is difficult not to love London as it is an exciting, multi-cultural and lively city that has something for everyone. However, be prepared to spend money as the cost of living is quite high compared to most cities. Public transport is widespread, if a little unreliable and the underground does not run for twenty-four hours a day. Rent is also expensive, although if you are prepared to live outside Zone 1, bargains can be found. Expect to pay £150 a week for a relatively basic room.

Visa and Work Permit Considerations
For non-EU residents, getting a work permit is relatively straightforward and an application for a twelve-month Tier 5 visa is usually processed in under two weeks. As a well as the application fee of £130, your London agency needs to provide a 'Certificate of Sponsorship' with a unique reference number, and while the application is being dealt with, you must stay in your country of origin. Be careful when filling out your forms as just one mistake can result in the Tier 5 visa being rejected by the Home Office.

London is a vibrant city, with a varied market that benefits from a strong currency.

MIAMI

The Market

Miami has long been a popular destination with both American and international clients due the pleasant winter weather, consistent sunlight and great locations. Therefore, every year from January to late April, models from all over the world make the trip to South Beach in the hope of shooting campaigns, catalogues, commercials or at the very least building up their book by working with some fantastic photographers. However, castings are always very busy and in recent years the global economy has affected the Miami market. The emphasis towards beachwear and lingerie work makes a good physique a must.

Tourist resort and millionaires' playground. Miami Beach is a heady mix of sun, sand and sin.

Paris is a feast for all the senses.

are sights to be seen and if you lose your way, most Parisians speak English. The cost of living is very expensive, but with a little endeavour, you can easily hunt out bargains. The atmosphere in Paris is warm, although the locals view the flocks of tourists that descend on the city each summer with an air of condescension.

Visa and Work Permit Considerations

Obtaining a visa to work in France is specific to your country of origin. For example, EU residents require no visa and Canadians can take advantage of the working holiday visa as long as they are between the ages of eighteen and thirty and have not participated in the programme previously. Americans, however, cannot take advantage of this type of visa and are required to pay $94 and apply for a long-stay visa. Speak to your agent.

SYDNEY

The Market

Sydney is the fashion capital of the Australasian market and subsequently can be both a chance to shoot high-profile as well as well-paid work. Australia as a country places a heavy emphasis on health and well-being and

therefore models are expected to be in peak physical condition.

The Lifestyle

The year-round warm weather and surfer culture in Sydney make this city a very relaxed and enjoyable place to live. Furthermore, it is full of cafés, juice bars and gyms, adding to the healthy lifestyle most people enjoy. The cost of living is comparable to many other cities and there are a host of model apartments and short-term rentals available on and around Bondi Beach. Sydney has a large gay and lesbian community and Mardi Gras is a unique and memorable experience. In summary, the centre of the city is very cosmopolitan and Sydney has something for all.

Visa and Work Permit Considerations

The Australia Working Holiday Visa, also known as the WHM Visa, allows entry and work in Australia for up to two years. Models can take advantage of this facility, but you must be between 18 and 30 years old, have a valid passport with at least one year until renewal and be able to provide evidence of sufficient funds to support yourself when you arrive in Australia.

Sydney is a cosmopolitan and energetic city with an ideal climate. Aussies are fiercely proud of it.

TOKYO

The Market

Tokyo has a consistent amount of commercial work throughout the year, with the exception of a ten-day holiday in April for Golden Week. The demand for inter-national models from major department stores and fashion firms is high, particularly for lingerie and under-wear work. Tokyo is also known for having a strong editorial market, along with many more high-profile magazines that frequently book international models.

Tokyo – unique and energetic.

alternative representation is a big step and should never be a knee-jerk reaction to a quiet couple of months. Also, the way you go about switching agency is a sensitive issue, making it extremely important not to make enemies or burn bridges.

Firstly, if you are considering changing your agent, then examine why you feel this change will help. If it is a personal issue with a booker, you are unhappy with the agency as a whole or you are not convinced of the direction your career is heading, seek an appointment with your agent to air your thoughts and gauge their response. Your agent might not even be aware of the problem and without bringing it to their attention, a solution will not present itself.

You should also consider what an alternative agency would offer, as well as if you should make changes to your own approach as a way of improving the chances of getting booked. If your thoughts still point towards a change, then be as open and honest in the transition as possible. Many bookers from varying agencies communicate either professionally or socially. Talking to another agency without being diplomatic can result in offence and may cost you a contract.

Overall, don't seek to change your agent without thought, care and a justifiable reason.

BRANCHING OUT

Success as a model often leads to opportunities that, if grasped, can open the door to an array of exciting and alternative career paths. There are many examples of film and television actors, presenters, agency directors and fashion show producers who all used their time in the modelling industry as a vehicle to branch out and explore other careers. By preparing for these possibilities and then approaching them with the same vigour and professionalism that you bring to your modelling work, you can take further control of your career and prove yourself to be even more versatile and adaptable than ever. One of the main perks of working as a model is the flexibility of your schedule, meaning fewer time constraints when attempting to branch out. For example, in the same day you could attend a casting for a photo shoot, have a screen test and still have time for an afternoon dance class.

ACTING

Models choose to go into acting for many different reasons, but incorporating acting in your list of skills can broaden horizons, heighten confidence during commercial castings and improve the believability of emotions on camera. Furthermore, by using the initial exposure

When fashion meets theatre. Models with movement are always in high demand, making dance classes a useful tool.

provided by modelling, you can open doors into the film and television industry without necessarily training.

Firstly, it is recommended you attend an acting class, even if you're not planning to make the transition completely from model to actor. The flexibility of a model's schedule makes tuition a possibility, and in a very short space of time most will find an improvement in their on-screen performances. These improvements include everything from being able to take direction to the art of learning a script. At the very least, casting directors are impressed by models with a little acting experience.

If you wish to go further, ask your agent if they have an acting division or a connection to a commercial acting agency. If you do have separate agencies representing you, it is important they communicate, so be honest over how you hope to divide your time, your level of commitment and where you see your career heading. You can begin by representing yourself. There are websites and forums dedicated to announcing castings and auditions for actors either with or without an agent. Attend a couple and see how you get along.

Actors are advised to join the acting union or guild in their country of residency. Unions protect the rights of performers and negotiate minimum terms and conditions of employment bearing in mind the current economy. Being a member of such a union will also secure your stage name, allowing no other performers the right to the same name. Unions offer free legal advice and support in disputes over professional engagements, free advice on tax and are even willing to give advice on non-union-based contracts. Most unions offer accident insurance to their membership. Each union has an informative website showing what they offer to their members.

If acting is something you are hoping to go into, then there are many things to consider. However, by taking some basic courses, you can disprove the theory that models cannot act and book a catalogue of well-paid commercial work.

DANCING

Being able to dance is surprisingly useful for models. Many photo shoots require graceful movement in front of the camera and action shots will translate better onto camera if a model has great control over their body.

Therefore, dance classes are suggested as a way of improving confidence, ability and an understanding of music. These are particularly useful for fashion shows and producers are more likely to cast models who can dance or who are able to pick up choreography with a level of ease.

Some pop videos and commercials also require a range of dancing skills, which can be anything from sensual freestyle and gymnastics to classical ballet and ballroom. At these castings a casting director may just want to see if a model can move with confidence in front of the camera, whilst others will want a model to perform a routine.

Overall, dance classes are not only beneficial for models wishing to hone their skills and expand their repertoire, but for fitness, body toning and socializing. If you have a talent for a particular style of dancing, inform your booker so they can add it to your list of skills. Dance experience or training is always seen as positive; your agency will be delighted with your versatility.

PHOTOGRAPHY

Moving behind the camera is not uncommon for models and makes sense considering the wealth of experience they can acquire on set. If photography is something you are interested in, then speak to the crew about techniques and other models about testing. How much you spend on your first camera is a personal choice, but it is advised to hone your craft on less-expensive equipment and move up from there.

SINGING

Being a confident singer can often be beneficial to a model; it is surprising how often models are called into castings where they are casting alongside singers for the same job. Television commercial and pop video castings sometimes require a model to sing; often the model's voice will not actually be used, but a confident singer will be able to lip sync convincingly, breathe in the right places and show a degree of musicality when phrasing.

As a model you might also receive some exciting castings, opportunities to sing backing for famous music artists or perform alongside celebrities. Once again, being a model and having the right look can open doors.

Casting directors like to work with people who are

Other models are only too happy to test with someone hoping to move into photography.

interesting and talented, so being able to add singing to your list of skills will only heighten people's interest and increase your chances in a casting. Being a keen singer shows you're extrovert and have confidence in yourself and your performance.

Always have a song in the back of your mind that you could sing unaccompanied and that will show off your voice. Think about the interpretation as well as the sound; by doing so, your performance will have depth and be believable. Sing something that represents you.

TELEVISION PRESENTING/HOSTING
Being a presenter is very different from being a model and yet many presenters have made the transition from the photographic studio to the television studio. This is because the elements of both presenting and modelling are similar. A good look is useful and when mixed with qualities like confidence, approachability, intelligence and an understanding of how to develop a relationship with the camera, the leap from modelling to presenting does not seem that great. However, live hosting is not straightforward and the reason that truly good presenters make it look so easy is because they possess the ability to combine faultless delivery of lines, from either an autocue or pre-prepared script, whilst considering timing and the producer's direction via an earpiece. Even pre-recorded pieces to camera require a degree of multi-tasking and the need to accurately deliver the information with focus, personality and spontaneity. Of course, these are skills that can be learned, and with enough practice even the most daunting of tasks can be overcome.

If you have a genuine interest in becoming a television host, compère or presenter, then, just like modelling, you need an agent to represent you with potential clients. Some model agencies have divisions that deal with this type of work, but having an agent that only deals with presenting is likely to benefit you in the long term. Acquiring an agent requires as much research as when you first found your model agency, and be wary of any agency that asks for money in advance. Send them a biography highlighting your interests, skills and why you feel you're an ideal candidate for a career in television. Most importantly, you need to include a showreel that demonstrates your ability to be relaxed, likeable and versatile on camera.

Your showreel should be three to five minutes long and be in either a DVD or CD-ROM format. The case it comes in should have a clear head shot on the front, which acts as a nice introduction, and if you can fit your biography on the back, then overall this will make a nice package. However, try not to fixate on the perfect showreel because the sooner it is seen, the sooner you can gain representation and work.

A common misconception is that a showreel needs to consist of several examples of professional presenting work. Obviously, as your career blossoms your showreel will increasingly include examples of work, but, just like your modelling portfolio, your aim should be to give potential agents and clients a snapshot of who you are

Parenthood changes lives, but having a baby can open doors in your career. Infant and maternity modelling is an ever-growing part of the industry.

Hosting at trade shows and live events is great preparation for television presenting.

and how effectively you perform on camera. Therefore, when making your first showreel, make sure you include an introduction, a section of you talking to camera and examples of you interviewing people. These interviews need not be with celebrities or elaborately produced and can be as trivial as asking people in the street about their opinion on popular culture. The purpose of these is to display your ability to interact with others whilst still maintaining control of the interview. Above all, letting your personality shine through on your showreel will catch the viewer's attention.

In summary, presenting is an enjoyable way to supplement the income you receive as a model and can develop into a career of its own. However, there are limited spaces available and lots of young girls and boys hoping to forge a career on television. Be sure to document every piece of presenting you do. Finally, don't give up if a

showreel doesn't work for you. You can always start again. And remember: the more time you spend on camera, the better you'll be.

In summary, acting, singing, dancing, presenting, photography and becoming a make-up artist or booker all integrate well with a modelling career. Whether you see these as a new challenge, an additional revenue stream or as change of career, there is no doubt the skills learnt will aid you as a model.

FINANCE

Having longevity in the industry is not only about making money, but also managing it. When dealing with your finances, there are three major areas to consider: your short-term finances, annual taxes and long-term investments. However, whilst it is possible to deal with each issue separately, the attitude you develop towards your daily money management will directly affect your annual profit and the taxes you are legally required to pay. Then, at the end of the financial year, the cycle begins again, and with care, you can begin to factor in longer-term investment projects. However, it is vital to understand that there are no financial guarantees for self-employed models and every month you must earn your desired amount or adjust your living expenses accordingly. An unhealthy attitude towards money quickly results in a downward spiral of debt, which can be the end of even the most promising career.

As soon as you sign your contract with your model agency, you should do three things. Firstly, notify your tax authority of your intention to work as a sole trader, then open a separate business bank account with its own debit card, and finally find an accountant to help prepare your annual tax return.

TAX

It is an inescapable part of life that everyone has to pay taxes. Whilst those working for companies have their tax automatically removed from their salary, as a self-employed model it is your personal responsibility to report to your tax authority your annual income. This amount is considered to be the sum of all the money you receive for work as a model, including photo shoots, fashion shows, usage buyouts, recall castings, travel day rates, and so on. However, as well as your income, the business costs you incur in the pursuit of that income are also taken into consideration before the amount of tax you are legally obliged to pay is calculated. These expenses are referred to as being tax deductible, and for models there are very specific and unique guidelines about what you are able claim as an expense. For example, the food you buy is considered to be tax deductible, but only when you are away from the city or town you live in as a result of your business. Even then, to claim your food bill as an expense, you must be out of town overnight. Furthermore, different countries have their own legislation, which can change annually as new tax laws are introduced and existing ones are altered.

Also, by referring to your home as your office, a percentage of your utility bills are considered to be tax deductible, but this percentage depends on the number of rooms in the property excluding bathrooms and kitchens. From these two examples, it is immediately apparent that tax law is a complex and dynamic field, making it best to find an accountant who has experience working with models. Discuss, in detail, what, when and where you can declare an expense, because by understanding how the system works, it is possible to minimize your tax bill. Here is a list highlighting expenses that you should consider deducting from your annual income.

Be sure to declare your entire income and never make false expense claims. If the tax authority investigate you and find your finances to be erroneous, you will be fined and made to pay the unpaid taxes and you could face a criminal prosecution.

YOU AND YOUR ACCOUNTANT

Having an accountant has many advantages. As well as correctly filing your tax return and liaising with the tax authority on your behalf, they are knowledgeable about current legislation and ways to drastically reduce your annual tax bill. They also provide information about longer-term tax strategies, which again can save you thousands. However, the real bonus is that the cost of the accountant is, itself, a business expense. Therefore, the money spent on an accountant would have otherwise been a part of your taxable income, and

Show me the money! Work for your money and then let it work for you by speaking to your accountant and a financial advisor.

I know a model who ...

has never paid tax or even registered. She was prosecuted and can't even open a bank account.

Tax Deductible Checklist

- Business assets: cars, composite cards, computers, envelopes, portfolio, stamps, stationery, and so on
- Beauty treatments and dental work
- Clothing used for stage purposes
- Gym membership
- Hotel rooms
- Household utilities bills
- Interest on business loans
- Make-up and beauty products
- Hair cuts
- Out-of-town food
- Phone bills
- Test photography
- Travel expenses: planes, trains and automobiles

so, accountants provide value for money. Nevertheless, once you register as self-employed and hire an accountant, your goal should be to keep your daily records and receipts accurate, up to date and easily accessible to ensure that, at the end of the financial year, you and your accountant spend the least amount of time possible preparing your tax return, as this can affect the fee they will charge you.

Your accountant will request a sales figure, which comprises your total income for the financial year, including fees which have not been paid by the year's end and commissions deducted by agencies. These should be set out in a spreadsheet detailing the corresponding invoices and the dates that monies were received. Also, a spreadsheet of all business expenditure incurred in the year is required. It should be divided and sub-divided into categories, again detailing the date, amount and a brief description of each expense item. Be sure that all supporting invoices are referenced. As well as an expense spreadsheet, list separately any business assets purchased during the year such as computers, office equipment or even a car.

In addition to the spreadsheets your yearly bank receipts need to be analysed in order to verify your claims. List your banked fees, interest and other miscellaneous items as well as banking expenses separately. Lastly, if you have any credit card statements or cash expenses a similar exercise would need to be undertaken on a separate spreadsheet for each.

In summary, speak to your accountant about their pricing structure and how you can save them time, and yourself money, because the less time they spend drawing up your accounts, the lower your bill will be. One last advantage of employing the services of an accountant is that banks prefer a professionally produced tax return as evidence of your earnings and this could affect how easily you secure a mortgage or business loan.

BUSINESS BANK ACCOUNT

Having a separate business bank account helps to draw the line between your personal and professional expenses. From this account you should set up a standing order to a savings account, which should be equivalent to a third of your monthly income. This money now represents your annual tax fund and should only be accessed in extreme circumstances. Although tax authorities are willing to listen if you encounter financial difficulties, you will be expected to pay your tax bill in full and on time. A separate savings account ensures you are not struggling when the bill arrives. Any money left over after the bill has been paid can be used towards expanding your business. For example, use it to cover the initial cost of travelling to a new market.

In summary, the money you earn is yours to spend in any way you choose, but remember that a percentage must go to the tax authority. Also, there are no guarantees about the size of your next pay cheque, which means you need to always have at least a month's worth of living costs in hand. Models who don't look after their money soon fall into a hand-to-mouth cycle by which the money they earn immediately vanishes and they are again relying on future work just to stay solvent. Instead, plan, react and adapt your lifestyle to ensure growth and financial security.

Final Thoughts on . . . Remaining on the Main Board

I think forty-year-old women actually look more healthy and fit than some girls in their twenties. I've met women who have way better bodies in their forties because they've been working on them for all these years.

Claudia Schiffer

Capitalizing on successes year after year is not an easy task, but by nurturing your client base and managing your money, you can build a secure foundation from which to expand, travel and try new things.

A Final Thought

The reason we wrote this book was because we believe that every model's chance of success is firmly within their grasp and by understanding there is much more to modelling than most people think, you can take control of your career and get ahead. Whilst it is important to remember that you are not competing with other models at castings, it is your job to convince potential clients to book you and then keep booking you. You won't book every job, but by having a great look, book and attitude, you can significantly improve your chances.

Once you gain a good reputation and a strong client base, you'll feel confident and secure when approaching new clients and markets and the more successful you become, the more this feeling will grow. What's more, like most things in life we enjoy what we are good at and modelling is no exception. This enjoyment becomes infectious and clients and crew will gravitate towards your good vibrations, allowing you to create a positive environment wherever you go. However, regardless of how much success you enjoy, never become complacent and feel you have all the answers. Even after twenty years' combined experience, we are both still learning new things every day.

If things aren't going according to plan, then stay upbeat and always communicate with your agent, because it is just as important to form a close relationship with your booker as it is to find a good agency. Always remember that you are both playing for the same team and one phone call can change everything.

Finally, although the demands of modelling are not easy to share because of the way society views models, modelling is one of the most fun ways to earn a living imaginable. Having said that, it *is* a job, so always take your work, but not yourself, seriously.

The future of the industry now lies in your hands and we would wish you luck, but as you will soon see, luck has very little to do with your success!

Where to Now?

After reading *The Model's Handbook*, you should have all the tools to develop a great look, book and attitude. But what now? Well, why not find us online for daily videos, interviews, articles and advice on how to get the most out of a life in front of the lens. Our website www.themodelshandbook.com is the place models go to for up-to-date tips on improving general health, learning yet more tricks of the trade and getting to know the community. Also, if you feel a modelling career is something you'd relish, but you're still hesitant about contacting an agency directly, then send your photos to talent@themodelshandbook.com and we'll do our very best to help.

There are also competitions and giveaways, recommended products and plenty of opportunities for you to contribute to the website and quickly become part of themodelshandbook.com family. What's more, there are forums for you to air your thoughts.

If you have any questions for the authors then please contact us:

julian@themodelshandbook.com
fiona@themodelshandbook.com

You can also follow us on Twitter: @modelshandbook. And remember to check out our Facebook page.

Glossary

above the line work – fashion, high street or runway modelling; the more glamorous and highly paid end of modelling

below the line work – work that isn't seen by the general public, but can still be lucrative

best age models – more mature models

bookers/booking agents – people who work in a division of a model agency. Each booker has several different clients/models

buyout – a set fee that allows the client to use the image as often as they wish

catwalk/runway models – highly paid models who showcase fashion designers' clothes

composite cards – collection of images showing a model's look and measurements, used as a marketing tool

cover ups – concealing body make-up

crashing a casting – attending a casting that you haven't been invited to, because you think your look will fit

fit model – model who works with a clothing company to ensure their samples are best fit and quality. Not to be confused with fitness models

general casting/cattle call – a time when clients look at all the available models around, which generally lasts a whole day

go-see – an appointment where models are interviewed by people in the industry

ident to camera – prior to taping a television commercial, this is a chance for models to warm up on camera, give their name and details and talk briefly about their hobbies or studies

location house – site of a photo shoot where the sets are not 'real', but have been created

look book – seasonal shots from a company, showing key outfits, on location

mother agent – company or person who introduces models to the industry

on option – models placed on a shortlist for a job

rates – the amount per hour, day or half day, that models are paid

tear sheet – page from a publication showing a model's work

television commercial casting (TVC) – a filmed casting for a client, who may or may not be present

usages – fee agreed, according to how long the client wishes to use the image, and how prominently the model features

voucher books – used in America, three-part vouchers that confirm the details of the job including working hours and the day rate

Z-cards – also known as composite or comp cards

Index